LIVING IS NO LAUGHING MATTER

A Primer on Existential Optimism

Michael Hogan

ISBN: 9798695046571

Published simultaneously in the Republic of Mexico and the USA in cooperation with Fondo Editorial Universitario and the American School Foundation of Guadalajara, A.C.

Publisher: Fondo Editorial Universitario

Cover design by Mike Riley, Ajijic Books Publishing.
www.ajijicbooks.com
https://www.facebook.com/ajijicbooks/?ref=bookmarks

Ordering information:

Directly from the author at
http://www.drmichaelhogan.com/index.php OR

on Amazon, in Kindle or paperback.

Library of Congress Cataloguing information:

Hogan, Michael, 1943—

1.Addiction and recovery. 2. Combat high. 3. Concentration camps.4. Existential optimism. 5. Meaning of life. 6.Memoir. 7. Prisons and prisoners 8. Philosophical essays. 8. Spirituality.

3rd edition: March 2021

2nd edition: December 4, 2020

Contents

"It's when I'm weary of considerations,
And life is too much like a pathless wood
Where your face burns and tickles with the cobwebs
Broken across it, and one eye is weeping
From a twig's having lashed across it open."

—*Robert Frost*

"I've found that the best way though pain and loss
and grief is to find purpose."

—*Joe Biden*

For Gary Hogan, who died too young, but who lives each day in my heart and is reflected in the eyes of every student I have taught.

DE LA SALLE

The French words literally mean "of the classroom" which provided the eponymous name of our school, De La Salle Academy in Newport, Rhode Island, and also identified the Christian Brothers who taught there. They had founded their order on the principles of St. Jean Batiste de la Salle, a French Catholic missionary in the New World. I don't know much about Jean Batiste, but I do know that my own life has been pretty much defined by the classroom and that I continue to help others define their lives through my vocation as a teacher. I was thinking today about how that happened. Such a vocation was remote from my early experiences as a student. I was often the class clown, the troublemaker, the one who in the days of corporal punishment always got the ruler across the knuckles, the yardstick across the butt, the short humiliating slap to the cheek.

And yet… I was a better than average student with honor roll grades, an enthusiasm for writing, public speaking, and the question "why." I also managed to find a mentor or two along the way: Sister Mary Carmel in 4th grade math, Brother Dennis in 9th grade English, Peter Lucchesi in Freshman Comp at college, and Richard Shelton and Steve Orlen in graduate work-shops at the University of Arizona.

I suppose the defining year was in 9th grade when, weighing in at 150 pounds on a 5'10 frame, I decided to go out for the football team. I'm not sure what the reasons were but among them had to be the fact that my father had played football, that it was considered the manly thing to do, and that I had spent the summer previous isolated from my peers and feeling disconnected from life. Football seemed to me to be a kind of answer, an external force or energy which would push me in a direction (any direction) and relieve me of an unshaped, un-motivated, directionless adolescence. I had a lot of testosterone flowing, I remember. My sexual life was non-existent outside of *amour propre*, but it was not from lack of trying. I had a great deal of bottled-up aggression as well, and no way to safely release it. So, there I was this skinny kid trying out for the JV team and not even knowing what each position was, as the oth-er boys shouted out where they wanted to play and began shap-ing up a scrimmage team. Quarterback, halfback, fullback, end, guard. And now here was the coach. A former linebacker from Boston College, an imposing six foot something, 200-pound bulk of muscle not yet slackened by the daily grind of teach-ing social studies at a Catholic high school. *What's your name?* Hogan. *Do you know how to snap the ball?* What? *You know, hike the ball?* Oh yeah, sure. Figuring: how hard could it be? And then at the end of the week, after practicing hundreds of snaps and rising up to block and getting my neck pounded and my head slammed into the ground, learning precisely how hard it was, and how much my precision would come to be depended on. As the season progressed I learned how a team was only as strong as its center, and that I was not as good as I should be and never would have the physical strength to be as good a cen-ter as the team needed. But unfortunately, I was it; there was no other. So, I made myself the best I could be both at that position and at middle linebacker on defense by adopting strategies which earned me the nickname "the crazy white boy." I realized rather quickly that the only thing that could make up for a natural deficiency was a determination far beyond that of most teenagers, a willingness to take chances, a refusal to quit, and a dogged aggression that was relentless and a bit insane.

The next year I was first-string varsity, and the next, until in my senior year in the opening round robin game, a benefit to establish a fund for injured players, I was blindsided by two opposing blockers and suffered a severe concussion and internal hemorrhaging. Well, I knew then that my vocation was not to be a football player. And within a month had taken to hanging out with the street gangs, smoking cigarettes, drinking beer, joyriding around the island, making out in the back seat of my dad's car with public school girls, coming in late, going to school with a hangover. At a pep rally for the Thanksgiving Day game I was given my third varsity letter by the coach and received a standing ovation from the entire student body of both our school and our sister school, Saint Catherine's. I was a wounded hero, *hors de combat*, sidelined by superior forces, but still the crazy white boy, dangerous and eminently dateable. Senior year was party time.

As a result, although I was wait-listed, I did not get into Harvard and had to settle for a small liberal arts Catholic college in New England where I was fortunate to receive a small scholarship. There, philosophy replaced football and I became obsessed with two things: the first was a rational basis for my loss of faith, the second, a search for the meaning of life. I found one professor and one student with whom I could have deep and meaningful conversations. I had a couple of girlfriends who were generous with their time; I drank copiously as often as I had money or a rich friend to accompany me to Boston nightclubs or Cape Cod retreats; read even more copiously, and began what would be a lifetime's search for meaning.

Philosophy was my major, but the courses I was forced to take fit me like somebody else's pair of pants. While my search for meaning was liberating, I found the translating of Aristotle and Thomas Aquinas boring, and the systematic decoding of Kant and Hegel tedious and confining. Dr. Ernst Royal, my philosophy professor and advisor told me one day: "You should look into creative writing as an option. You are an imaginative young man with a great deal of passion and talent. But I don't think you have the discipline for philosophy." I knew he was right and didn't argue. I changed my major and never looked back.

Well, that's not entirely true. It took some time, but I did look back, as I continue to do so today with this book. While I changed my major, I kept philosophy as a minor, and I continued in a less-than-systematic way to search for the meaning of life. This search and my writing have been two of the three greatest obsessions in my life. The third obsession, after more than three decades in AA, has been held in abeyance.

I discovered that at some point in my search for meaning I'd have to return to the philosophers I'd found too tedious, boring, or *cymini sectores* ("splitters of hairs"*)* in my undergraduate days. I'd have to read widely and critically, but most of all I'd have to draw on my own experiences and begin to make sense of them. Clarity was the most important thing, so the alcohol had to go. Also, relationships which were frivolous, and distracting were replaced by one woman, a few quiet friendships, and a great deal of solitude. It was within that solitude that I began to examine my life. I began to decide which were my strengths and which my weaknesses, which aspects of my character I could change and which I needed to accommodate myself to and work around. In the process of doing this I found that no philosophy that attempted to define the meaning of life could be universal unless it was like a piece of cloth which was cut, trimmed and sewed in the pattern of an individual life. I was becoming what might be known as an existentialist. However, it was not the existentialism defined by Jean Paul Sartre but rather a more refined, eclectic and workable version which began to infiltrate itself into my teaching, my interpretations of literature, my writing, and the pattern of my life.

Two things stand out in the evolution of this new philosophy. The first is a small book by Victor Frankl. Frankl was a survivor of the Nazi concentration camps who had to discover a philosophy of life that was rational, that had positive psychological elements, and that could be translated into a survival skill. In other words, he set out to articulate a philosophy that not only made sense but was pragmatic; one that actually worked in daily life. I would draw rather freely on his ideas and yet also enlarge upon them based on my own needs, circumstances, and experience.

The second contributing factor came about through playing tennis and from my reading of Abraham Maslow and his rendering of "peak experiences." To formulate a philosophy that kept one alive and could be translated into a survival skill, was only half the battle. A philosophy which affirmed life was important. But it was not enough. I wanted more than that. I wanted the feeling of ecstasy, the feeling of transcendence, the feeling where one is both outside oneself and deep within oneself, living so deeply that every movement is full of grace.

I read books about the mystics: St. Teresa, St. Francis, St. Catherine; books on Zen Buddhism, the New England Transcendentalists, as well as Eliot's "Four Quartets" ("the moment in and out of time") enough to be assured that the experience was real. Interestingly, on the tennis court, as I played with the intensity that once characterized my abbreviated football career, I began to actually experience it for myself. This feeling was liberating, this feeling which sports psychologists now call "the zone," that place of total focus where one is playing with such absorption that one becomes a part of the flow of the game and the ego disappears, and it is the doing, not the goal, which is important.

I wondered if one could live one's life like that. If one could take an existential philosophy, combine it with focused activity, and live a life which would be productive, moral, useful and meaningful. There was only one way to find out and that was to go ahead and do it. To begin to utilize these ideas and techniques in a holistic way. The result is what I now describe in this little primer as Existential Optimism, a philosophy which has a rational and academic base but is pragmatic and can be used in day to day life. A philosophy which utilizes the best of current psychological knowledge as well as personal experience; a system which, quite simply, works. Will it make you a happier person? Will it make you a richer person? Perhaps. But more importantly it will make you more fully you. The only real tragedy in life is the one Thoreau was concerned about when he went off into the woods at Walden and that was "to discover at the end of your life that you had not really lived."

This book is addressed to those who realize, in the words of Nazim Hikmet, that "living is no laughing matter," and that this millisecond of illumination in the darkness of eternity is too precious not to live as freely and as fully as possible.

THE FIRST PLATEAU

Every summer in the Sonoran Desert grown men and women die of thirst, overexposure or sun stroke, often within a few miles of the nearest town. When such a death occurs, the newspapers editorialize. *If your car breaks down,* they warn summer visitors, *stay by the vehicle, conserve body liquids, and wait for rescue.* Yet, each year the warning goes unheeded, and each summer more feckless visitors die.

I spoke with one man who had survived being lost in the desert, one who followed the survival instructions. I asked him what went through his mind when he found that he was lost, stranded in the Sonoran wasteland. He told me that his first thought was "This can't happen to me. I'm a civilized man in a civilized country." The possibility of his death enraged him, and he could hardly resist the impulse to march double-time across the desert in search of help. But he stayed fast. He knew that the nearest town was much further away than it seemed, even if he could guess the right direction. He also knew that to underestimate the debilitating effect of 140-degree ground temperature and the angry Arizona sun would be fatal, so he stayed with his crippled vehicle.

Hours went by without a sign of rescue. A night passed. The furnace blast of another morning arrived and still no sign of search planes or rescue vehicles. "Did you despair?" I asked him. "No," he replied. I asked why he did not, since his situation did not seem particularly hopeful. "I did not despair," he said, "simply because I chose not to."

He was found after three days, a bit dehydrated and with a new respect for the desert, but in reasonably good health and quite strong. His comment about "choosing" not to despair struck me as both unusual and simplistic. Did one really have a choice in the matter?

A friend of mine who is an artist and having a rather difficult time with her work wrote to me recently and said: "I sometimes think: what difference does it make anyway? The whole planet will eventually be swallowed up in the black suck-hole. And what does it matter? The suck-hole takes Schweitzer just as surely as Hitler." An interesting view and not all that uncommon.

I suppose the man in the desert, if of a certain philosophical bent, might have had the same thoughts. He might have just stretched out beneath a saguaro cactus and melted in the sun. But he was neither a philosophical man nor a religious one, as far as I could ascertain. Yet, he was a person of faith. Such people come in all sizes and shapes. The well-known Arizona poet, Richard Shelton, who built his home on the edge of the desert, writes in his book *Chosen Place*:

> the inevitable consequence
> of a well-directed life is death
> and the inevitable consequence
> of a misdirected life
>
> is also death
> at night I keep telling myself
> go to sleep nobody is to blame
> we are what we are

the world is as it is

And eventually I go to sleep
But I never believe it.

Shelton is, of course, a poet. There are for him no easy creeds, no consolations available from traditional religions. Nor, looking across his stark desert world can he find any solace, any reason not to despair, any hint that life—in the final analysis—is not absurd. And that is because, quite simply, there is no reason "out there." As Shelton tells us: "Living in the desert/has taught me to go inside myself/for shade." For those who are neither fortified by the old credos nor convinced by the external reality that there is any reason for hope, this inward retreat is vital.

John Paul Sartre writing in *Being and Nothingness* observed that there "is no such thing as human nature, simply because there is no God to conceive of it." He thus broke with the Aristotelian dualism of essence/existence which formed the intellectual basis for most Christian theology. Perhaps a brief review of that would be helpful here as we get the underpinnings of Existential Optimism in place.

Aristotle believed that everything in the world has existence (that which is) and essence (that which makes a thing what it is). He held that essence preceded existence. An architect first conceives a house (essence) and then the house is built according to his blueprints with bricks and mortar (existence). This, he argued, is true of all created things.

Sartre agreed up to a point. He submitted that a thing had to be thought of before it could be created, but that this applied only to artifacts, i.e., things created by man, since only man was capable of thought. After he exists, then he creates (or fails to create) his own essence. He defines himself through his own authentic acts or fails to define himself.

Along with this notion came the thesis that life was inherently meaningless. Having no purpose beyond that which he chose to invent, subject to all the accidents of fate regardless of how he tried to define himself, man became an absurd figure in an indifferent cosmos. Given a brief span of years in which his own body and its processes worked to betray him, made the sole arbiter of the rightness of his acts, living merely by chance, existing for no apparent reason and for no end of any significance, man found himself alone in the universe, naked, frightened and despairing. Fred Turner, a contemporary poet of great perception writes:

> Right here where does one go from now?
> Huge things have come and gone…
> It had always been a life
> In which one could so to speak
> Lay up treasure in earth as well as heaven…
> Now it is different.

This tremendous freedom of being in charge of one's life, this wonderful deliverance from the bondage of worn-out creeds and archaic philosophies is also seen as a great loss. "This great capacity," says Turner, "is great emptiness."

But it seems that, having reached this point of enlightenment, one still has many choices. One can go back to the world of Aristotelianism and once again embrace one's childhood faith. It is atavistic and intellectually repugnant to some, but for others there is a tremendous emotional satisfaction in such a withdrawal. It is certainly one of the choices available.

> Maybe if I were a child again…
> or could go crazy…
>
> The world getting bigger and bigger
> then I would play and float,
> then the sun would blaze again
> then the distance would burn up with light.
>
> The net of logic opens
> and shuts again.

Having come so far it is impossible for most of us to simply go back. It is simply not one of the options available. This poem, entitled "Maybe," written by Miklós Radnóti, goes on:

> I would be a child, but memory hurts.
> The nettles sting like splinters in my tiny fingers.
> And the leaves grow high on the mulberry tree.
>
> Or maybe I would be a nice madman
> And live in the yellow house high among yellow
> Flowers, with a small bell around my neck.
>
> But I just look around. The ditch is here.
> I walk and think, then walk again
> And wait for longer and longer winters.

This poem was written by a man who spent years in a Nazi concentration camp. He died there, thrown into a mass grave.

When he wrote this poem, death was only a few months away. His position was absurd, contradictory, and sad. His intellectual maturity would not allow him to become a child of simple unquestioning faith again. He had too firm a grip on reality to go insane. The prospect of death, the even bleaker prospect of life in the prison camp was horrendous. Yet he chose to face the reality of his existence unflinchingly. And that is the first plateau.

DEATH OF A CHILD Part I

It was 1992 and my wife and I had been teaching at a school in Guadalajara, Mexico for two years, enjoying the climate, the people, and the students. Lucinda taught junior high of the American School and I taught in the high school. I had recently been selected to be the department chair and had begun to make major changes in the curriculum. I loved my work and was excited to upgrade the academic offerings. Life was good. Our house was only a few blocks from the school, and we welcomed the greetings of neighbors, "Buenos días, Maestros!" as we walked along the tree-lined streets each morning to work. It was a blessed time. Lucinda and I enjoyed our colleagues' company as well as the companionship of a lovely golden eyed Doberman we had rescued from the pound. Life was good.

Then, on an otherwise uneventful Monday, I got a call from Colorado that my only son, Gary, had died suddenly. He was 27 years old and in the prime of life. Like all such deaths it was meaningless, wasteful, absurd, and pointless. He was charming, intelligent; he was warm-hearted, eager and enthusiastic. Though he had a few setbacks in the past and some problems with substance abuse, he had been getting back on track and had shared with me his ambition to be a historian and perhaps teach at a university someday. He wanted to be a history teacher, and nothing I could say about poor salaries, low prestige, and long hours would dissuade him. But he died before his dream could be realized. After the grief, after the heartache, what shape could I give this death? I had no answers. His death left me bereft and rudderless. But each day when I arrived at school our principal, Miss Soledad Avalos, gave me a warm and heartfelt hug. She was a spiritual woman with a generous, caring heart and was known by students and faculty alike as "Miss Sol."

Still, as the days went by, I realized that I had no inner resources to cope with my son's death. I was estranged from his mother who lived up north, and my new wife did not really know Gary, so her well-intentioned words of comfort rang hollow.

I came close to breaking down in class one morning and decided that I would submit my resignation from the school and return to the States. When I sat down with Miss Sol, I opened my heart to her. I expressed my gratitude for the trust with which she had endowed me, for the promotion to department head, and my regret that I could no longer work at the school as a teacher. I was simply too emotionally distraught and did not think I would be able to continue. She listened patiently and sympathetically. Then she got up and wrapped me in a warm hug that lasted more than a minute. I was not used to such intimacy from an administrator and was at first uncomfortable and pulled back. But she held on tight, and gradually I experienced a sense of peace and comfort.

When she resumed her seat, she told me, "I am so sorry for your loss, Michael. And I can only begin to imagine the depth of your grief. I have never lost a child. But I have lost someone whom I loved dearly, and I know that being around people who care for you, who love you, is important. Here at this school you

have come to be loved, and we consider you as part of our family. The students know that you are suffering and will bear with you. The faculty, too, have shared with me their hope that you will come out the other side of this painful experience and continue to work here. But I fully understand if you wish to leave.

"I would only add this. You are a very good teacher. One of the finest I have worked with. But you could be a truly *great* teacher if you could begin to see your son in the eyes of every child you teach. It would transform your classes into something special. You would leave a legacy which would be remembered for a long time. So please, for my sake, and the sake of those children, take a day or two to think about it. Talk it over with your wife and then go to a quiet place, maybe say a prayer, and then come back to tell me what you have decided."

We stayed. For more than three decades now. And that is the meaning I have chosen to add to my view of the world: to see the face of my son in every child I teach. I know we heal each other by our willingness to risk the hug, the openness, the sharing of our feelings, and—in the process—we come to see our son in everybody's son, our daughter in everyone's daughter. If I have come a long way from that day in graduate school when I was a competent but indifferent university lecturer, if I have grown to be worthy of the highest title I know: *Teacher*, it is because I have flown quite literally on the wings of my son's love. Together, Gary and I and my family and my extended family at the American School, have reshaped and redefined the meaning of our world. Each day I have the reminder from Miss Sol that in the face of every child I teach there shines the face of God.

"EVERYTHING YOU LOVE WILL LIKELY BE LOST... "

—∽—

One of my favorite writers is Franz Kafka. Most of his tales are a bit surrealistic and only hint at meanings which the reader must expend a bit of effort to find. Certainly, his best known works, *The Metamorphosis*, *The Trial*, and *The Castle*, all reflect an absurdist view of the world in which forces beyond the control of the protagonist quite overwhelm him and reduce him to a pitiable figure, tossed this way and that by the bureaucracy, the military, the forces of nature, indeed by life itself.

Kafka had no children of his own but one day when he was out walking in the wooded park of Steglitz in Berlin, he came upon a young girl of seven or eight who was crying unconsolably because she had lost her doll. Helpless, the mother stood by wringing her hands. She had suspected the girl had been playing close to the woods and had lost the doll in the acres of high grass where it was almost impossible to find. Kafka offered to help the child and mother look.

After an hour or so of futile searching, Kafka had to leave for an appointment with his editor. But he promised the girl and her mother than he would return the next day and help her look again. He kept his promise. Once again, they looked assiduously. Once again, they had no success. The doll was indeed lost.

He came back the next day and helped the girl search. But still no luck. So, after a lunch break when Kafka disappeared for a bit, he returned with a letter. He said the missive was from the doll herself, and she had written it for the little girl. The note said, "Please do not cry, I have gone on a trip to see the world. I'm going to write to you about my adventures." Thus, began a series of letters and stories which would continue for several years. Each time he and the girl met, he would read to her his thoughtfully composed letters of the adventures that the doll had experienced as she travelled around the world. The little girl was enchanted and looked forward to each one.

Finally, Kafka read her the last letter. This time the doll told of her return to Berlin, and with this final story Kafka gave her a new doll that he had purchased. The little girl was puzzled. She complained, "But this does not look at all like my little doll!"

Kafka handed her another letter. This one said, "I know I must appear different. My trips, they have changed me." The girl nodded thoughtfully, then gave both Kafka and her new doll a hug.

Many years later, long after Kafka died, the girl now grown-up found another little note tucked into a crevice in the doll. The message, signed by Kafka, read, "Everything you love is likely to be lost. But in the end, love will return in a different way."

THE SECOND PLATEAU

I do not underestimate the impact of pain, isolation, sickness and degradation on the human spirit or on one's ability to reason. My own life experiences have given me a great deal of respect for men like Miklós Radnóti, in the concentration camps, who managed to simply confront the reality of their situation, grit their teeth, and walk stolidly toward likely death. But I believe that we are capable of more than that. I believe that it is possible, regardless of our circumstances and even the negativity, or worse, *indifference* of others, to do more than simply confront reality and muddle through the day.

Heize Piontek observed wryly: "You can shoot sparrows out of the sky/But can you force them to fly in only one direction?" Perhaps. Given enough time and the kind of fortuitous occurrences that would enable a roomful of monkeys to type the Gettysburg Address. My experience has been, however, that no matter how pervasive the negative effect of one's environment, one can still, if one chooses, live authentically and with occasional delight.

There is a poem by William Stafford which is about clarity

in the darkness; it is about ritual which will provide structure, and it is about speaking clearly and simply to one another (no matter what the occasion) of those things we know but do not often articulate. It is called appropriately enough "A Ritual to Read to Each Other." It goes like this:

If you don't know the kind of person I am
and I don't know the person you are
a pattern that others made may prevail in the world
and following the wrong god home we may miss
our star.

For there is many a small betrayal in the mind,
a shrug which lets the fragile sequence break
sending with shouts the horrible errors of childhood
storming out to play through the broken dike.

And as elephants parade each holding the ele-
phant's tail,
but if one wanders the circus won't find the park,
I call it cruel and maybe the root of all cruelty
to know what occurs but not recognize the fact.

So, I appeal to a voice, to something shadowy,
a remote important region in all who talk:
though we could fool each other, we should consider –
lest the parade of our mutual lives get lost in the dark.

For it's important that awake people be awake,
or a breaking line may discourage them back to sleep;
the signals we give – yes or no, or maybe—
should be clear, the darkness around us is deep.

This is an important poem for me, especially the reference to the darkness around us, and about the clarity of the signals we give to each other, and how important that clarity is. William Carlos Williams once said, "You can't get the news from poetry, but people die every day from lack of what is found there." I also like the Stafford poem because of its title: "A Ritual to Read to Each Other." We need to be reminded and we need to remind those around us through ritual, through daily ways of touching, that we are part of a loving family and a loving community; it is how we rescue one another.

Some time ago I saw a woman in Texas being interviewed after the execution of the man who killed her daughter. At the end of the interview the reporter asked, "Do you forgive him now that the execution has been carried out? Can you finally let go of this man who killed your child?" The mother replied, "I will never, ever forgive him as long as I live." Beside her were two other children, ages six and ten, who were listening to what she said. So, who was she hurting? The murderer had been executed. He couldn't be hurt any more, at least in this world. She had refused to create meaning, refused to define what had happened in her own terms, and by that refusal she allowed the murderer's power to prevail; she allowed negativity and destruction to flow through her and be passed on as a legacy to her children, a legacy of hatred and resentment.

Once Jesus was asked how many times we should forgive our enemies. They said, "Master, it is written that we should forgive our enemies seven times." (Next time someone denigrates teachers, remember how Jesus was called again, Maestro, master, teacher.) Anyway, this particular teacher said to forgive our enemies not seven times only, but seventy time seven times! 490 times? Talk about a tough homework assignment! Even in a good marriage that's tough! Seventy times seven times. Obviously, he was not speaking for the good of our enemies. He was speaking for the good of our own souls, our own psyches, so that we would not be poisoned by the hatred and negativity of others. It was basic psychology, Psyche 101 in Jerusalem. Picked up by the psychologist William James at Harvard 1900 years later. Eliminate the trappings of organized religion if you will from your school curriculum, but don't throw out the wisdom of the ages, the literature, the philosophy, the psychology available in those classic works which tell us how to save ourselves and our children, how to survive in the dark night of the soul. The darkness around us is deep.

There is a ring to Beelzebub's defiant speech in Milton's *Paradise Lost* as, condemned to an eternity of darkness, he proclaims: "The mind is its own place and can in itself/Make a Hell of Heaven or a Heaven of Hell." I do not suggest that the will should so abscond with thought, or imagination should so color reality that one convinces oneself that prison is freedom, death is life, or hell is heaven. That would be self-defeating. It would be a failure to acknowledge and build upon the great evolutionary leap that the existentialists made in facing up to reality and to the first plateau that we arrived at in an earlier chapter. Moreover, such an act of will—in addition to being regressive and an intellectual cop-out—could lead one to an acceptance of the lowest forms of human degradation. No, I do not believe that one should practice such self-deception. What thrills me as I read those lines from Milton is this: without any reason for optimism, without any apparent hope, Beelzebub simply chose to live optimistically. In doing so he created opportunities for self-actualization which could not otherwise exist; he was now open to possibilities which despair by its very nature would have closed to him. And I believe it is possible to do this without self-deception, and without the evil genius of a satanic will.

What I am writing about has more to do with attitude, with one's stance in the world, than with speculative reasoning. Speculations without attitude are, for the most part circular. It is attitude which gives them form, and some attitudes more than others lead to elegant forms, greater leaps, and higher levels of awareness.

There is a difference between attitude and expectation. Attitude is a way of going: expectation, a wishful demanding.

Alan Watts speaking once of human expectations said that we should expect good things as we might expect to find a letter that we are commissioned by a friend to pick up at the post office. If the letter is not there, we are not angry. We simply report that fact to our friend: "The letter was not there: perhaps tomorrow it will arrive."

But let me return to Beelzebub before I get too far afield. I noted that it was his choice, which was significant. With no apparent hope, with no reason for optimism, he *chose* to live optimistically. While not ascribing much value to the deception he practiced upon himself to do it, I do think the choice is worthy of comment.

Suppose you were informed that in ten years this planet would spin out of its orbit into a black hole in space. Would you live the next ten years in a state of chronic anxiety? Or would you hide out in a cave somewhere and refuse to see anybody. Would you abandon your work, cease learning, forsake good food and drink, and leave those you love? Or would you commit suicide and be done with it right now? These are after all some of the options that are available. But why choose them? Why focus on the black hole and not the sunflower? Why savor the metallic taste of despair instead of embracing what is here now and living intensely in the time that is available.

Any life, whether lived in the ghetto, a Park Avenue apartment, a maximum-security prison, or a cabin at Walden Pond, contains infinite possibilities. Because one cannot compose a symphony, perform open heart surgery, have sex with a film star or go to the moon, one is not less of a human being than those who can. Each of us is unique, with his or her myriad capacities for development, for experience, for growth. Each of us has an imagination, and the *active imagination* (not to be confused with fantasy) has creative power. As Pablo Picasso once noted, "Everything you can imagine is real."

A friend, with whom I once found myself in very difficult circumstances, once told me that my cheerfulness was quite annoying. He asked me why I chose to be so optimistic in the face of a very oppressing reality. Why? Well, why not? It was not the world that was disheartening, or even his circumstances in it. Rather it was his choice to be disheartened in that interior world which he created every day. He allowed himself to indulge a momentary feeling so that it coalesced into an attitude.

Although it may appear true, it makes little emotional or spiritual sense to say that life is meaningless. It is a passive and uncreative observation. It is more productive and truer to say that we have at this point chosen not to invest it with meaning.

If our life is merely a millisecond in the "darkyears" of space, why then let's savor it, let's embrace it, let's see it clearly while it lasts. If it breaks us, if it leaves us old and crippled, well—that's the way of life—no one gets out alive anyway. But let's not break ourselves. Let's choose to be life affirmers.

And this is the second plateau. Having faced the reality of life with our eyes wide open, we choose to affirm it, to flow with it. We choose to believe in our own self-actualization regardless of where we find ourselves. In choosing to be fully ourselves, we outwit the witness universe.

DEATH OF A CHILD Part II

When my son, who was a lovely, kind, brilliant, and ambitious young man in his twenties died suddenly, I was devastated. His death was abrupt, meaningless, and left a gaping hole in my psyche that I knew would never heal, never scar over. For days I was numb, unable to work, to think, and went about my teaching duties in a haze. Teaching did keep me sane, though. I focused on the young people I was working with and learned to see my son in each of their faces. I suppose along the way I was becoming a more compassionate, more accessible teacher, and was certainly available to students after classes in a way I had not been before.

Spiritually, however, I was bereft. I hadn't completely lost every scrap of faith, remnants remained, but they were too fragile to be of any solace. Philosophically I was at the lower end of Sartre's definition of existentialism. Life was meaningless, absurd, and the death of a child was one more piece of evidence to prove that. But I also knew that holding on to this belief was not life-affirming, neither was it a philosophy which I as a teacher felt would inspire or motivate my students. It was a philosophy of despair, a philosophy calculated to depress rather than uplift, to tear down, rather than to build upon.

In the midst of this storm of spiritual negation I was asked to attend a funeral Mass of a colleague whom I did not know particularly well. At the funeral, a Jesuit priest gave the sermon in Spanish. I was still in the process of learning the language, so I was often distracted when listening to long narrations in a second language. This priest, however, hit upon just the exact note that resounded like a Chinese gong in my consciousness. He said that when someone we love dies, especially someone young and who was in the prime of life, we often say; "*Por que?* Why? Why did this happen? Well, if we were truly honest, what we really are asking is "Why did this happen to me? Because it is how the death affects *us* that we are really speaking of. The person who has died feels no pain, no regret, no remorse or hope for tomorrow. It is those of us who are left behind who are asking this question in the bleakness and hopelessness of our deep sorrow and loss. *Por que? Por que?* What has this happened to me? Why has this person been taken away from me? Why am I left with this hole in my heart, this emptiness in my stomach, this bleakness of everyday life?

But the better question, he went on to say, the question that we should be asking, the question that can change us and thus change the world, is *Para que?* What can we make of this death? How can we create meaning out of this meaningless loss? For we are the authors of meaning, not God, not fate, not the universe with its millions of galaxies streaming through space indifferent to our sorrows, our needs, and our terrible losses. So, *para que?* What can I do to make sense of the senseless? What unfinished task did the departed leave behind which I can finish? What thought or inspiration did he or she have that I could emulate? What dream unrealized that I could fulfill? And when we find this, when we find a way to give that death a meaning, we will discover not only that the loss has

become a more bearable part of our memory and everyday consciousness, but also that your loved one lives through you in a way that is both empowering and life-affirming, and you have given to the departed soul a bit of immortality.

PARA QUE?

My son Gary loved studying history and all the elements that made up that discipline: chronologies, geographies, cultures, literatures, evolution of armaments, and political philosophies. His goal in life (never to be realized) was to become a historian.

After listening to the priest talk about *para que?*, I began to think about how my son's wish might relate to my own life. As a writer I was used to doing research, both to create fictional characters, and for the occasional nonfiction article. However, I had never done any extended work in history. When I received an appointment to teach at a school in Mexico, however, I discovered that one of my forebears had been a combatant in the Mexican Army resisting the US invasion of 1846. He was a member of a group called the Battalón de San Patricio, a military unit primarily composed of Irish immigrants who fought on the Mexican side. I knew little about the group and there was only one published historical work on the battalion in English, and a short novella in Spanish. I read that material and searched for more. I realized that I would have to explore Mexican records of the 19th century, as well as visit the US and Irish archives. It was more work than I was willing to take on, since I was teaching full time and chairing two departments.

However, with my son's death and this new incentive from the priest's talk, I began to firm up a commitment to begin that work in earnest. I realized that I needed a broader background in Latin American history before I could get anywhere, as well as a better knowledge of the Spanish language. So, I enrolled in courses at the Universidad de Guadalajara. That was the beginning.

During spring break and over the summer months I visited all the battle sites of the Mexican War. I interviewed descendants of the original battalion. I conducted research in the Archivos de la Nación in Mexico City, as well as the newspaper archives (Hereroteca Nacional de México) which housed the 19th century daily and weekly journals. When our school introduced Week Without Walls, I had the opportunity to accompany a group of Mexican students to Washington DC and visit both the National Archives and the Military Archives there. Although I discovered a treasure trove of materials at the latter, I was unable to take the time to copy them since most were stored in boxes and not filed in any orderly fashion. Plus, since I was responsible for a group of students, I could not spend my time in Washington on personal matters.

When I explained my predicament to the archivist in charge, he sympathized and took down my personal information. Two months later, he called me and said that he had put all the records on microfiche and would send them to me for a nominal fee. What a wonderful response and what a teaching moment for my students! As I told them at the time, when you do your work quietly and persistently, unknown friends will find you and angels will surround you.

The next year I had a similar moment when the archivist at the Museum of Interventions (Museo Nacional de Intervenciones) allowed me free access not only to their archives, but their storage cellar in an old convent that was the locus of one of the last battles of the war. There I discovered a cache of American weapons (smuggled by Guatemalan gun runners after a burglary at Harper's Ferry) which had been hidden for over 150 years! Meanwhile, I continued my courses and, three years later, had a doctoral degree in Latin American history, a competency in Spanish, and a dissertation entitled "The Irish Soldiers of Mexico" which was rich, not only in the factual history, but in compelling narratives gleaned from my research.

I sent queries out to major publishers and finally one accepted my manuscript. After a year working with the editor, expanding, verifying sources, obtaining permissions for photos, re-working some of the academic language to a more popular narration, the manuscript was finally a book that we both agreed would be a major contribution to US, Mexican and Irish history. But when the time came for publication, I was notified that the marketing division of the press projected that it was a "niche book" and, without a major buy-in from the Texas Board of Education, the largest purchaser of history texts, it would sell only a few thousand copies. They decided not to publish. I was devastated.

But here's the thing. I truly believed that this was my son's legacy. I felt that this work which his death inspired needed to be accessible to a wide audience. Consequently, I was only momentarily discouraged, then the resiliency of purpose set in. That evening I went to a poetry reading at the University of Guadalajara and ran into an editor by the name of Emmanuel Carballo. When he asked if I was working on anything new, I told him about the "Irish Soldiers of Mexico" manuscript and my trials with the publisher. He offered to read it, and a few weeks later called me to let me know that he was excited about its possibilities as a book and he thought it should be published. However, there was one problem. Lack of funding. He said

I needed to get a *patrocinador,* or co-sponsor, for the Fondo Editorial Universitario to publish. He suggested that I give a presentation to the Heróico Colegio Militar, an organization similar to the West Point Alumni Association in the US but composed of Mexican general officers. If they were interested, perhaps they would underwrite the project.

Well, imagine! A gringo high school teacher giving a presentation in Spanish on Mexican history to a group of Mexican senior officers. How intimidating! But with my son's image in mind, I did so humbly yet enthusiastically. To my surprise, not only were the officers enthusiastic about the project, they also provided a translator, a retired brigadier general to translate the work to Spanish, and also offered their facility for the formal book launch in later that year.

And so, the unimportant niche book that was supposed to sell only a couple of thousand copies, sold out its first printing in less than 90 days, then went on to sell twelve editions in English and three in Spanish. It was a best seller on Amazon and held the #1 spot on Mexican history (and Irish history) for several consecutive weeks. Even now, thirty years later, it continues to have brisk sales. It was an inspiration for four documentaries, an MGM film starring Tom Berenger, and a commemorative postage stamp from Mexico and Ireland. I have since been invited to speak at all the major universities in both Ireland and Mexico on this little-known aspect of their mutual histories, and I am a consultant to the embassies of both nations.

Even more important, the book prompted a closer relationship between Mexico and Ireland, resulting in scholarships for Mexican students wishing to study in Ireland, increased trade between both nations, (including the purchase of Mexican cement for use in Irish construction), Irish dance schools in Mexico, a mariachi group in Dublin, a popular music CD by the Chieftains, and a solidarity between both nations which contin-

ues to this day. *Para que?* What meaning could I possibly create from my son's death. What might result from the attempt? The blessings far exceeded my fondest hopes. This inauspicious book dedicated to my son resulted in bringing two nations together and formed a solid bond of international friendship resulting in increased educational and business opportunities, cultural exchanges, and a feeling of good will. *Para que?*

THIRD PLATEAU: THERE IS ANOTHER WORLD AND IT'S IN THIS ONE

The next several chapters will examine altered states of consciousness and how they can contribute to the formulation of the philosophy of existential optimism. We will look at such phenomena as runners high, "in the zone" experiences, flow, focusing, meditation, mindfulness, and epiphanies, most of which have truly positive physiological as well as psychological benefits. They relieve us of anxiety, quiet our fears, and clear our minds of petty troubles and concerns. Even more importantly, they remind us that there is another state of being aside from ordinary consciousness that we can tap into and that can deepen our appreciation of the profundity of existence. These experiences almost always involve an element of self-forgetting, the abandonment of ego, and the sublimation of self to a higher consciousness. In sports we find that we are capable of performances far beyond our ordinary ability; in the creative area we find ourselves inspired and thus writing, acting, painting, or otherwise performing at a much higher level.

While all of these are relatively healthy pursuits, they do have some hidden risks. They sometimes cause depression when we return to our normal state. Almost every actor has experienced an emotional let-down after a series of successful performances. Writers feel it most acutely when they are going through writer's block after having had a good run. Athletes know it when they are in a slump. Sometimes when one is in this depressed state, the temptation is to find a way to relieve the tension, the depression or the frustration. It is this that can lead to less healthy pursuits.

Another risk is feeling that one would like to prolong this state of higher consciousness and, if it cannot be achieved by the activity that originally produced it, then to search for alternative ways. This is especially dangerous for addictive personalities.

So, we will also look briefly at other induced states of altered consciousness which include: the adrenaline rush, the combat high, use of alcohol and drugs. For most of these the dangers are obvious but what is less apparent is how much at risk those people are who have already experienced the natural high and are no longer able to experience it due to physical injury (in the case of athletes), or loss of inspiration or creative energy in the case of artists, and the ten percent of people who are simply genetically predisposed to addiction.

The Third Plateau is simply this: Having had a unique experience, we become aware in the words of the French surrealist, André Breton, that "there is another world, and it's in this one." We suddenly realize that we are capable of achieving a high level of performance, an increased feeling of well-being, and even an awareness that might be defined as "spiritual," in which the body along with its pains and limitations, as well as the conscious mind with its doubts and preoccupations, are submerged into a higher consciousness. It is quite amazing and

can lead us to a higher level of thinking and living. Once the doors of perception are opened, the possibilities are endless.

But there is a caveat. We would be less than human if we did not want to prolong these moments, to replicate them again and again. Herein lies the danger. *For it is not the moment itself which has the life-changing significance. It merely hints at the possibilities that lie before us if we patiently grow into a life which prioritizes a higher level of consciousness.* The experience itself is merely a moment of awakening. What we do with it will dictate how we change, grow, and define our lives and those around us.

RUNNER'S HIGH, IN THE ZONE, AND FLOW

—⟋⟋⟋—

My daughter, Melissa, is a confirmed runner who can be found most mornings on the trails and foothills of the Colorado Rockies. She also writes for magazines which embrace the sport and where often one may read articles about the phenomenon called "runner's high." This is a type of euphoria many runners experience when they reach a plateau or second wind, and is accompanied by the release of endorphins that make them feel like they are moving effortlessly, almost floating, and could continue cruising along for miles.

Generally speaking, it occurs only when one has been at it for a long time. Beginning runners usually do not experience it. The reason is that you need to get past the level where you are just slogging along and thinking about how much longer until you finish your run. You need to build your endurance and get to the point where your mental focus and energy is no longer on the running itself. Where your muscles and breathing have taken over the task, and the brain has reached a tranquil state of self-forgetting.

Thus, sometimes—not always—and never in a predictable way, you can pass over into an almost mystical state where you have somehow managed to escape the self; where the blue of the sky is more intense, the air blissfully fresh and full of oxygen, the track and its surroundings more vivid, and your body almost weightless as you glide along. Marathon runners are more likely to experience this—especially at sustained levels—than short distance runners.

While early research once attributed this phenomenon to the release of endorphins in the bloodstream and their effect on the brain, this appears to be only a partial answer. The endorphin upsurge helps reduce pain, exhaustion and muscle ache, but it does not provide the euphoria which is the actual high. New research at the University of Heidelberg appears to have discovered the missing element. Scientists there have determined that it is a combination of endorphins and cannabinoids which results in the runner's high. The second chemical, of course, is found in marijuana.

The good news is that you don't have to be a long-distance runner to experience a similar rush of euphoria. Swimmers can also experience this, as can bicyclists or anyone engaged in a strenuous cardiovascular workout.

In the Zone There is another phenomenon which is also often referred to as "flow," or "in the zone." It is a metanormal capacity which professional athletes (and sometimes amateurs) achieve from time to time. Anyone who has observed football players, such as the Patriots' Tom Brady, knows that when a quarterback is in the zone, he is able to avoid defenders, visualize the entire field, and pinpoint his passes with unerring consistency.

Some running backs are so instinctively aware when in the zone that they can elude six or seven tacklers by fakes, spins, and the ability to follow blockers or find holes where none existed seconds before. Some receivers when in the zone can catch passes with one hand, tightrope the endzone line, and land perfectly time after time after time. The legendary Texas, A & M quarterback Johnny Manziel ("Mr. Football") and his favorite receiver Mike Evans are classic examples of this extraordinary ability and have been memorialized in the collegiate record books as well as on YouTube.

This uncanny ability has been written about in almost every sport: golf, tennis, basketball. Everyone has seen the basketball star sink three-pointer after three-pointer when in the zone, while on another night his performance might be just average or even mediocre. We have all seen the golfer making the bogey under pressure, or the tennis player coming back from a losing game with lobs, net volleys, and slams, and impossible shots to win the set.

Many books have been written about this phenomenon. One of my favorites, *The Zen of Tennis,* reflects my own experience as a tennis player. I first began playing at the age of twelve on a macadam court at a public park in Newport, Rhode Island. My coach was a retired army colonel in his sixties, called affectionately by the name of "Pop" Flack. He taught the geometry of angles, how to use the whole court, how to approach the net and make winners. I had no natural talent in the sport, so he also gave me a few tricks such as drop shots and slices. Mostly my game is 3.5 or a decent club game. I am not a gifted player and have no particular strengths, but I have continued to play over the past six decades and have found opponents in over thirty countries who were kind enough to give me a game or include me in their tournaments. I love the game and I have found that when I forget everything else and just focus on the game itself, I sometimes cross over to that state where muscle memory carries the game and I make the perfect return that, if I had taken the time to think about it, would have been impossible. It is this self-forgetting, this dramatically altered consciousness which puts me in a flow where I am capable of performing far beyond what my 3.5 classification would dictate. And I sometimes end up astounding—for a few moments at least—not only my opponent but also myself.

At those times I am fully present in the moment, totally focused. Nothing exists outside of the geometries of the court, no bodily needs, no pains, no muscle aches, no thought of winning of losing, only the flow of the game in which I am a mere conduit for the ball, an instrument, a faceless, egoless, embodiment of energy.

Now here I am in my seventies, older now than Colonel Flack was on that summer morning when he took a skinny twelve-year old out to the concrete courts of a seaside town to give him the gift of lifelong victory. He gave me not only a way of maintaining both physical and psychological fitness, but also a way of moving with grace and a sure sense of gratitude. One of those ineffable spiritual gifts which continue to give again and again when I walk onto a sun-drenched court, go over to measure the net with my stick (a Wilson H-26 titanium racket), and all the world narrows down to the clear geometries of the white lines, to the sound of the thwock as the ball hits the strings, as my muscles respond again in their dependable way to the known rhythms of the game, and everything is suddenly whole and perfect, and the world completely intelligible.

ADRENDALINE RUSH

—ɷ—

Scientists have known about the function of adrenaline since its discovery by a Japanese chemist in 1900. It is stored in the adrenal gland until needed in a moment of stress. It has evolved as a necessary survival tool in humans as man was confronted by predatory animals. The release of the hormone increases the output of blood to the muscles, releases fatty acids as nutrients, and causes the lungs to dilate, thus facilitating more efficient breathing. All of these result in a rush which gives the brain clarity and the muscles more power. We have all heard stories of the mother who moved a car single-handedly to save a child trapped beneath it. It was only later that she discovered she had ruptured two discs in her back. Or the fireman who rushed into a burning building filled with smoke to rescue those inside and later was surprised to wake up the hospital with terrible burns and lungs full of smoke. Such superhuman feats are not only possible but more common than one would imagine. Such people not only perform seemingly impossible tasks but appear not to have experienced any pain during these strenuous activities.

It is important, however, to realize that adrenaline does not affect the brain itself. The term "adrenaline high" is a misnomer. It is the brain's perception of crisis, threat, or danger which comes first. The adrenaline rush begins in the brain. When we perceive a dangerous or stressful situation, that information is sent to a part of the brain called the amygdala. This area of the brain plays a role in emotional processing. As the danger is perceived by the amygdala, it sends a signal to another region of the brain called the hypothalamus. The hypothalamus is the command center of the brain. It communicates with the rest of the body through the sympathetic nervous system. The hypothalamus transmits a signal through autonomic nerves to the adrenal medulla. When the adrenal glands receive the signal, they respond by releasing adrenaline into the bloodstream.

The advantages of the adrenaline rush are apparent in times of crisis. It can improve our reaction time, helping us avoid automobile accidents at high speeds. It can increase strength and performance, as is seen by the example of the mother lifting the heavy car off her child. It can decrease our ability to feel pain as can been seen with the fireman who ignored his burns while recuing those trapped in a burning building

Some people actively seek out this adrenaline thrill though risky activity such as skydiving, bungee jumping off cliffs or bridges, cage diving with sharks, zip- lining, or whitewater rafting. Still others settle for more mundane attempts to induce fear (and hence the adrenaline rush) through activities such as watching horror movies, boxing matches, or riding roller coasters.

My purpose of including these types of experiences here is that they show a part of our consciousness which can reach to higher levels when induced by strong emotion. In other words, there is a *physiological* basis for the feelings and experiences of ordinary human beings when they transcend the boundaries of what the conscious mind usually considers possible. It is also

important to note that like any other power at our disposal it can be used for simply for pleasure, or to truly transcend our limited nature, and even to help others. Like any other power, it can also be abused.

THE THRILL OF COMBAT

—w—

Americans love to fight. All real Americans love the
sting and clash of battle. Battle is the most significant
competition in which a man can indulge. It brings
out all that is best, and it removes all that is base.
—*General George S. Patton*

When General Patton gave this speech to his troops
on June 5, 1944, he was making a generalization.
However, it was based on his own personal experience and that of many others who have fought in battle. Quite
frankly there are those who *do* love combat, who find it ex-
hilarating and who either did not experience fear when faced
with violent death, or who were successfully able to transform
it into rage. William James quotes a contemporary general as
saying, "… everything about [combat] attracts me, motivates
me, moves me, intoxicates me. I am crazy for it, I love it."

More modern examples abound. There are those who re-
enlisted for combat duty in Vietnam, and even more recently
in Iraq and Afghanistan when they had already experienced

so many horrors and witnessed such death and mutilations as would intimidate more pacific temperaments. Why on earth would they not only choose to do so, but do so enthusiastically?

In historian Joanna Burke's book on 20th Century warfare, she shows that even ordinary soldiers throughout history have had the experience of combat exhilaration. She relates how Captain Julian Grenfell a 27- year-old fighting in Germany during World War II wrote home to this mother that war "was the best fun. I never felt so well or so happy. The fight vitalizes everything, every sight and word and action." He especially enjoyed "pig-sticking" Germans after long period or inaction and boredom.

Marine veteran Jad Steinman interviewed several combatants who participated in post-9/11 conflicts in Iraq, Afghanistan, and Syria. He paid particular attention of those who had been awarded the Combat Badge and the Purple Heart. In other words, those who had not only been in battle but had good reason to remember it and the feelings it produced. Many talked about the "rush" they had experienced. Several had re-enlisted for multiple tours. One noted, "Somebody is trying to kill you. It is the biggest high you can experience.... There's nothing that will come close to that rush." It was something he actually missed now that he was a civilian.

One reviewer observed that "What really surprised me in this book was just the amount of exhilaration. "I wasn't expecting to see that, you know, in certain circumstances these men — often young men — got actually a lot of pleasure, a lot of exhilaration, a thrill out of the act of combat."

When they returned home to civilian life many would find substitutes for the thrill of combat by engaging in risky behaviors such as skydiving or free climbing. Surprisingly few of these men were psychopaths or even borderline personalities. Some were pilots who had fully adjusted to civilian life,

but who had experienced true joy and almost erotic excitement when shooting down enemy aircraft.

Others were infantrymen who spoke of brotherhood and comradery, but also laughed when speaking of a mortar hit on a position that wiped out an enemy platoon. They recalled stepping over scraps of corpses scattered by artillery fire or bragged about their marksmanship as they shot down the fleeing stragglers a hundred or more meters away.

"It is a rush like you cannot imagine," Marine veteran and Purple Heart recipient, Tom Valle, told this writer. "Although for obvious reasons most guys don't want to talk about it. When someone says to me, 'Thank you for your service,' I am tempted to reply, 'It was my pleasure.' But I restrain myself."

Many, of course, were not unscathed by the experience. Some of these men would have trouble adjusting to civilian life and would engage in criminal behavior. Others would or succumb to drug or alcohol addiction, suffer from post-traumatic stress disorders, or even commit suicide. As Robert E. Lee once commented to General Longstreet after the Battle of Fredericksburg, "It is well that war is so terrible, otherwise we should grow too fond of it."

ALCOHOL AND DRUGS

—⁓—

"For art to exist, for any sort of aesthetic activity or perception to exist, a certain physiological precondition is indispensable: intoxication."

—*Friedrich Nietzsche*

From time immemorial artists and writers have turned for alcohol or drugs to quiet their anxiety and self-consciousness and release the wider perception and flow which they believed a bit of alcohol could provide. Alcohol reduces stress, lowers inhibitions, and provides a sense of euphoria. It can also accelerate emotional responses. "No tears in the writer," Hemingway once famously wrote, "no tears in the reader." Hemingway, a devotee of booze it all its forms from wine to whiskey, considered it to be the only relief for an artist in a mechanized culture.

Nietzsche contrasted the force of the Apollonian which invokes reason, order and light, with that of the Dionysian which evokes the spontaneous, the emotional, the sensual. While structure and form might be important, he concluded that true greatness can only come when these are allied with passion, spontaneity, even ecstasy. Thousands of artists have followed this prescription from Francis Bacon to Jack London, from Vincent van Gogh to Jim Morrison, from F. Scott Fitzgerald to Amy Winehouse.

But there is a fly in this ointment of self-medication, or perhaps better stated, a worm in the tequila. Excessive use of alcohol can also dull perceptions, make one forgetful, deepen depression, distort reality, and decrease the ability to perform cognitive tasks. For those who are prone to addiction, and it appears that a large percentage of artists are (as well as at least ten percent of the general population), the results can be tragic. Loss of creativity and production, compulsive disorders, black-outs, anti-social behaviors, high risk activities such as driving under the influence, and indiscriminate sexual liaisons are just some of the unintended consequences. Continued excessive use can also result in liver disease, hospitalizations, imprisonment, seizures, and in the case of Hemingway, Dylan Thomas, Wine-house and millions of others throughout history, premature death. "First you take the drink, "F. Scott Fitzgerald wrote, "then the drink takes the drink, then the drink takes you." Many writers and artists would discover that the boozy "spirits" that they consumed drove out *the* Spirit, which was the true source of their inspiration and the engine that powered their art. With their souls emptied out, the fountain of their creativity dried up, and there seemed little to live for.

THE CORNUCOPIA OF DRUGS

From Thomas DeQuincy's *Confessions of An Opium Eater* to Aldous Huxley's *Doors of Perception* writers have searched for inspiration and transcendence through the use of drugs. More recent writers and proponents of psychedelics and hallucino-gens such as Carlos Castaneda and Timothy Leary attracted a large number of loyal followers. There is no question that, at least in the short term, some of these "worked" for a handful of artists, writers and spiritual seekers. This is especially true of the psychedelic drugs such as LSD (ergoline fungus derivative), psilocybin (magic mushrooms) and mescaline (peyote cactus). None of these are addictive and they have all been found to have properties which have been used in traditional medicine, and in the case of the psilocybin and peyote are used in religious ceremonies by native people throughout the Americas. Marijuana as well has been used by mystics, gurus, musicians, and poets as an aid to inspiration and release of creative energy. From Bob Marley to Willie Nelson, from Brad Pitt to Steve Jobs, the cannabis plant has been seen as a boon, not only for its release of tension and elevation to a euphoric state, but also for its medicinal benefits for people with cancer, arthritis and other degenerative diseases. The only caveat seems to be the lack of definitive research on the effect of these drugs on adolescent minds which are still formative. Preliminary studies seem to indicate that there is every reason to be cautious.

While opioids and amphetamines have garnered a much more unsavory reputation, especially in recent years with the opioid crisis in the Midwest and the extensive use of crystal meth throughout the US, it is important to bear in mind that they have legitimate uses and have been beneficial to many throughout history. Opioids have enabled people with excruciating chronic pain to go about their daily business and live productive lives. On the battlefield and in with traumatic injuries they have saved lives and enabled surgeons to do their work with a minimum of discomfort to the patient.

We all know the scourge of crystal meth which continues to be widely reported in the press. However, World War II pilots could not have overcome the furious assaults of German and Japanese pilots nor completed long-range bombing missions without the aid of amphetamines. Their use in providing short-term energy and maintaining wakefulness in terms of crisis proved invaluable. This drug is still used today by the military. Also, amphetamines have clinical use in the treatment of ADD as well as obesity.

Even cocaine which has among its other properties the ability to freeze the interior of the eye, has made possible ocular surgeries which would have been difficult, if not impossible, without that aid. Cocaine is also used during procedures involving the upper respiratory tract. In addition to anesthesia and vasoconstriction of the upper respiratory tract, cocaine also shrinks the mucosa or mucous membranes.

The danger of these classes of drugs lies in their addictive qualities. *Especially with people who are prone to addiction.* They take one Vicodin or OxyContin capsule to help with back pain and soon find that they want to take two or three. Or they use Adderall or Phentermine for weight loss and find that they are addicted to speed. Another danger is that when these prescriptions run out or get too expensive, the adults themselves often turn to street drugs which, adulterated with dangerous additives, can lead to overdoses and death. Equally troubling is the behavior of those youngsters who raid the medicine cabinet to experiment with the drugs that their parents have bought on prescription.

SEARCH FOR TRANSCENDENCE

—⟋⟍—

I t is important to keep in mind that whether the original reason the person used the drug was medicinal or what is commonly described as recreational, the underlying reason was to transcend the limits of the human body and mind. The opioid was used to mitigate pain. The amphetamine was used to extend wakefulness. The LSD was used to expand the mind; the psilocybin mushrooms were consumed in order to find a spiritual connection. In all of these cases, the goal was to reach a higher state of consciousness, a transcendence or (to use a word that has since been coopted by a designer pharmaceutical brand) to experience *ecstasy*.

And what is ecstasy but a higher state of joyful being? The search for ecstasy, "the pursuit of happiness," is a goal enshrined of the Declaration of Independence. The tragedy, of course, is that these shortcuts only give the user a glimpse of what is possible. As T.S. Eliot put it, "these are but hints and guesses." The lasting experience of transcendence demands more. It requires discipline, self-forgetting, and engagement with others, or at the very least a commitment to a higher cause then oneself.

The pathway of drugs alone leads to a dead end, psychologically and spiritually. And for many, in the throes of addition, to a physical end as well, as the histories of Kurt Cobain, Heath Ledger, Jim Morrison, River Phoenix, William Burrows, and a host of other artists, writers and musicians have proven time and time again.

Many physicians and treatment centers ignore the "search for transcendence" aspect of drug use and abuse. They seek to treat those trying to recover with more pharmaceuticals. They prescribe Antabuse or Vivitrol for alcohol withdrawal. They proscribe Methadone or Suboxone for heroin abuse. But they often find to their dismay that the subjects go on using again. Ask the addict on Methadone why he went out and bought heroin when he felt no pain of withdrawal, and he will tell you that he simply wanted to get higher. All Methadone did is take away the pain of withdrawal; it provided nothing but absence. What was missing from the life of the addict was precisely the element that was sought when he first began to use the drug. A movement away from emptiness to fulfillment. True recovery from any addiction, must provide this missing element, the absence of which was the underlying motivator of the addiction itself.

RECOVERY

—⟋⟍—

While the effects of abuse of alcohol and drugs as well as actual addiction have been explored here and reported in the press *ad nauseum*, there is another, more positive side, which is a part of our progression to existential optimism. That, of course, is recovery.

When a person in the unrelenting grip of addiction has finally "hit bottom," as they say, or has finally given up on a series of futile "attempts" to modify his or her behavior and just admits that will power alone is not enough, and surrenders, a remarkable thing occurs. The compulsion to drink or use is often lifted, and the person experiences a clarity and a freedom which is often described as miraculous.

William James, often referred to as the Founder of American Psychology, describes the phenomenon as "self-surrender," and this is reflected in the AA first step which is "Admitted we were powerless over alcohol and our lives had become unmanageable." But isn't that contradictory? If our life is unmanageable, and we are powerless, wouldn't we therefore go on drinking or using drugs? Aren't all bets off in terms of recovery? It seems not. It is one of those examples of paradox which contain an underlying truth; one that, while being experientially true, is also productive of conative dissonance. William James describes it metaphorically.

> You know how it is when you try to recall a forgotten name? Usually you try to help the recall by working for it, by mentally running over the person, places and things with which the name was connected. But sometimes this effort fails; you feel then as if the harder you tried the less hope there would be, as though the name were jammed, and pressure in its direction only kept it all the more from rising. And then the opposite expedient often succeeds. Give up the effort, think of something altogether different, and... the lost name comes sauntering into your mind...

Similarly, with addiction. Those who have been caught in the net of alcoholism, for example, have invariably attempted many different strategies when trying to quit. They switched from whiskey to wine. Or from wine to beer. Or they drank only on weekends, or after 4 PM. But soon they found themselves back to the addictive drinking. They tried exercise, or religion, meditation, or moving to another place, or changing jobs, or getting a divorce. As if their personal health, or habits, or their work, their mate, their geographical location was the cause of their problem. But nothing worked. They had promised family and friends that they would quit, but time after time they returned to the addictive substance, whether drugs or alcohol. Nothing worked. Their best efforts at will power had failed. They were muddled, hopeless, spiritually bereft, and almost insane with "trying."

The advice of James is the same. "Quit trying! Give up the struggle." Some hidden process was initiated during the struggle. Similar at least in principle to the search for the lost name, although far less trivial and much more life affirming. Once you had ceased trying and focused on something other than the lost name, once you had given up, and turned your will and your life over to the hidden force (a Higher Power) the result came spontaneously.

There is thus a conscious and voluntary way which works for some people who wish to quit drinking or smoking or disengage from any deleterious behavior. But for those truly addicted, willpower alone does not work. It has been shown time and time again. For at least 10% of the general population whom statistics state are prone to addiction, and who have tried and tried to quit, their case is hopeless. But give up entirely, and they will often find that the result will come of its own. "Stop trying and it will do itself."

The second step of AA is "Came to believe that a power greater than ourselves could restore us to sanity." Well, let's first of all look at the definition of insanity. It is essentially continuing to indulge in the same destructive behavior that has proven to be life negating again and again. Indulging in the same behavior over and over and expecting a different result is a form of insanity. "This time I will only drink after 4 PM and I will stop after two glasses." "This time I will drink only beer." "This time I will only smoke one joint before a performance." But each time the additive behavior rears its ugly head. Hard to admit, but it is a type of insanity.

Many have difficulty with the "came to believe [in] a higher power" part of this step, especially atheists or agnostics. But that should present no barrier to the open-minded who are serious about recovery. They certainly can admit that alcohol and drugs were both higher powers, leading them into behaviors that they did not voluntarily choose. We all know that we do not will ourselves to breathe when we are asleep or will our hearts to beat during the day. There are forces within both our minds and bodies which are stronger than our self-will. There are forces outside of us as well.

Through the self-surrender of the first step, we can access these forces. Remove the self-will, remove the ego, and the power of the group in recovery can come to your aid; your subconscious healthy mind will come to your aid, perhaps even a force which we do not understand and have no need to name will fill your life.

I remember my Irish grandmother who, when she lost some household item would often say this short prayer: "Dear Saint Anthony, look around. Something's lost and must be found." I used to think this was sheer superstition. Imagine busy Saint Anthony looking down from the heavens to search for my grandmother's thimble. Absurd. But, in fact, as James notes, a valid psychological process was at work here. Give up the conscious will, and you will find that subconscious forces are in fact doing what you were incapable of doing. Let the conscious mind do all it can in its power, then let go. The subconscious mind will take over. As James puts it, to continue "to excise the personal will is to still live in the region where the imperfect self is the thing most emphasized." More important than any theological issue, James assures us, is the pragmatic one. It works! Invariably, my Irish grandmother found her thimble which was in her sewing kit all along! And millions of hopelessly addicted people have been able to recover from the ravages of alcohol and drugs and not only lead exemplary lives but enrich the lives of others and help fellow sufferers to recover.

FOCUSING

—◊—

For many years I worked as a facilitator in creative writing workshops in prisons. These workshops were the only place where prisoners could express emotions without fear of reprisals from the administration, or violence from other prisoners. Practically all these programs, mostly run by volunteers, have been terminated as a result of overcrowding and more repressive incarceration policies. The noteworthy exceptions are the ones in Arizona and the San Quentin workshops in California, both of which have survived for over forty years and have boasted significant lower recidivism rates than the general populations in both states.

Most prisoners spend their time in a state of suspended animation with their feelings on hold. It is a common defense mechanism. When put into a maximum-security cell, the prisoner often feels remorse, a sense of personal worthlessness, sorrow, guilt, frustration and, when he contemplates the length (or indeterminacy) of his sentence, despair. John Paul Minarik, a poet in a maximum-security prison in Pennsylvania wrote:

In Kafka's short story "Metamorphosis" this George Samsa character woke up one morning from "unsettling dreams…and found himself changed in his bed into monstrous vermin." And the whole story is downhill from there, about his attempts to deal with the fact that suddenly he is changed into something odious. It is something like what happens in the courtroom after the work GUILTY, a sudden change which is thrust upon the person.

There are many ways to "do time" and one of them is to simply cease feeling by an act of will. The prisoner cuts himself off mentally from the world out in the streets, from his family, from those he loves. He severs the emotional ties. Games behind the wall occupy much of his attention: the daily scheming for drugs, cigarettes, better work gigs. Prison politics and prison gossip keep him busy and keep his mind off the world he left behind. And, if he no longer feels much joy in life, neither does he carry the heavy burden of sorrow, guilt, remorse and self-contempt which was laid on his shoulders when the judge said "Guilty" and the prison gates slammed behind him. He lives in a gray world of non-seeing, non-feeling, in which the days slip by quickly and nothing—not even a murder in the tier above him—is very disturbing.

I would hate to speculate how many men serve time this way. I know it is well into the thousands. Men who have chosen to see less, to feel less, to live at one tenth of their capacity for openness and sensitivity in order to maintain their psychic survival. What is ironic, however, is that the price they pay is psychic death. Just as the muscles of the body atrophy from lack of use, so does our capacity for empathy, for openness, for feeling, weaken and die when we fail to exercise it. And I think this explains in part why so many ex-cons commit crimes again and again after they are released from prison. It certainly explains why so many of their wives, who were loyal during their incarceration, divorced them shortly after their release. It also explains why they have so much difficulty relating to people outside.

It would be easy to blame the system for this kind of diminution of feeling. But, as I noted earlier, while the force of this type of environment is considerable and pervasive, one still has choices. How can one exercise them in such an environment? One way is focusing. Let me give you an example.

One of the members of the Arizona prison workshop, Charles Green, told me about the time he was out on the prison exercise field. He has been in prison then for about three years on a possession of marijuana charge. It was a dry barren place located in a desert plain below the Superstition Mountains. He had gone out on that field a thousand times and seen nothing except a few stabbings, the glint of the sun off the tower guard's carbine, the bored faces of his fellow inmates walking aimlessly around the perimeter. But on this one particular day, he looked at the top of the inside fence and observed the rolls of concertina wire. He looked more closely and saw two birds building a nest in the midst is the wire. In his prison journal he wrote:

> The birds flew back and forth, calling to one another, busy with their building. They were grey with a flash of chestnut underneath their wings—beautiful. I found out later that they were Inca doves and not particularly rare. Had the birds been here last summer or the summer before? I didn't know. All I knew was that this was the first time I had stopped to look, to think, to see, and be open to the world out there on the field. How sad that seemed. How wasteful. And who was responsible for that? Not the prison, not the men around me. The birds—just like the wall, the bored faces of the men and they tower guard—were all a part of my world. But by not focusing on them, by letting myself be overwhelmed by the forest and

> not searching out a single tree, I had cut off a part
> of that world, I had added another deprivation to
> those imposed by my captors.

With that discovery, however, came new knowledge. Charles Green knew with a certainty and clarity which he brought to our workshop sessions that he now had the power wherever he was to focus, to see things truly, and to experience even on the most oppressive days moments of joy, of light and beauty.

Working with prisoners and seeing this transformation cannot help but give the workshop coordinator a stronger and more positive outlook that informs his life. I have seen it in many of my colleagues who volunteered in this field including Richard Shelton, Joseph Bruchac, and Sam Hamill. When we return to our more sedate places where we teach traditional students after our work behind bars, we are sometimes seen as Pollyannas by our colleagues.

A gloomy acquaintance of mine whom I was trying to cheer up snapped at me one day. "Whoever said," he asked, "that man is supposed to be happy?" Well, I don't know. Certainly, I'm not saying that here. Being neither a professional philosopher nor a mystic, I don't pretend to know what a man is *supposed* to be. But I do know that if a person is capable of having moments of joy, then being joyful is part of what it means to be human. And if there are possibilities of experiencing beauty no matter where you are, then being human must consist—at least in part—of realizing those possibilities.

Because one lives in a degrading environment, or because there is much in our lives that is ugly, does not mean that we are under some kind of obligation to be miserable all the time. So, let me answer the question of my acquaintance with one of my own: "Whoever said man was supposed to be miserable?"

We have the capacity to choose to realize opportunities for joy, for inner clarity, and one of the ways we can do this is by focusing. Focusing is similar in some respects to what users of LSD in the Sixties called "tripping." It consists in isolating an object, contemplating it, concentrating on it as if you were seeing it for the first time. You experience the textures, the sounds, the smells, the vibrations, the colors of the object as fully as possible. You let your mind roam freely within the context of this experience. The pleasure that comes from this kind of tripping is intense, often mystical. It is a psychic force as uplifting as a crowded tenement or a prison cell can be degrading. As Oscar Wilde noted:

> Pleasure is nature's test, her sign of approval. When we are happy, we are always good; but when we are "good," we are not always happy. It is probable that the truth of this has never been understood, and that some men have remained savage and animal only because the world has sought to starve them into submission or kill them by pain, instead of aiming at making them elements of a new spirituality, of which a fine instinct for beauty will be the dominant characteristic.

Why is it that so many of us seem to prefer pain and boredom to joy and intense living? Well, for one thing it is not considered "cool" to find opportunities for joy when those around you are wallowing in misery. And it is not always the better part of valor to attempt to convince them that much of their misery is self-imposed. Also, in some situations the demands of reality are such that we dare not loosen our grip for fear we'll be caught unawares. And, finally, there is the feeling that we all have of being thought a fool—a fear of seeming naïve, silly, absurd, childish, even immoral. To return to Wilde again:

> So much has been surrendered! And to such little purpose! There have been mad, willful rejections, monstrous forms of self-torture and self-denial, whose origin is fear, and whose result is degradation

> more terrible than that fancied degradation from
> which, in their ignorance, they have sought to
> escape. There must be a new hedonism… its aim
> to teach man to concentrate himself upon the
> moments of life that is in itself a moment.

How delightful was the discovery that Wilde knew precisely what I was trying to describe and that the process of focusing which I thought was original, was actually the process by which many writers and poets create their magic and are able to instill in us, when we are open to them, a sense of true wonder. And it is this sense of wonder, more than anything else, which makes me a man of faith.

I am very much aware, in the moments Wilde speaks about, of the energy and mystery of the cosmos. I see that meditation, mindfulness, prayer, and poetry are all ways of attempting to arrive at a quiet place where one can experience those energies and mysteries. Some are more suitable than others to certain situations, but each is an attempt to deal with those energies.

What is perhaps most difficult is the state of intellectual tension (often physical and emotional tension as well) that one must live with the more one knows, the more one understands.

It is easy to surrender one's mind to this or that institutionalized notion of the deity and simply avoid questioning such notions. But it is also easy **not** to believe in these versions of the deity and go no further. The latter is the position of many college sophomores, and especially the sophomoric graduate students of philosophy. But if you open yourself to the moments provided by focusing, you can suspend your disbelief. You can approach both flowers and plants with the same sense of wonder that a child has. You can see that everything you have learned about them is merely limiting, merely descriptive. Explanations ultimately explain nothing.

So, it is possible to be a person of faith, not out of superstition or laziness or fear, but out of wonder. To see that life is a miracle, that the world is full of magic, that whatever one learns or discovers will never be enough, but that sometimes it will be more than enough. This acceptance allows one to believe in all the contradictions and see that in their oppositions lies some inkling of what the truth is.

Of course, the bottom line of this kind of credo is a belief in oneself and a trust in oneself to make these evaluations. One must do this with great seriousness but also with a sense of humor. For if this is sometimes productive of great arrogance, it must also be productive of great humility, an awareness of the tremendous fragility of being human as in Eugene Guillevic's poem:

> Whatever's not in stone
> Whatever's not in walls of stone and earth
> Not even in trees,
> Whatever trembles a little
> Well, that's in us.

Sometimes one finds that intellectual honesty requires one to reject the gods of his ancestors, in addition to the gods of his culture. The result, if honest, can give more true strength than a passive acceptance of either, as in Joseph Bruchac's poem, "Canticle":

> Let others speak
> of harps and
> heavenly choirs
> I've made my decision
> to remain here
> with the Earth.
>
> If the old grey poet
> felt he could turn and
> live with the animals
> why should I be too good
> to stay and die with them?

And the great road of the Milky Way
that Sky Trail my Abnaki ancestors
strode to the last Happy Home
does not answer my dreams.

I do not believe
we go up to the sky
unless it is to
fall again
with the rain.

Poets in our culture (for those who read them attentively) are more and more being seen as mediums, exquisitely sensitive tools for focusing. This is the poet as priest, performing the miracle of transubstantiation in pieces called, quite accurately, "epiphanies," that is, manifestations, pure clear moments in which one feels that he has gone outside the fabric of time. It is as if one has plugged into the cosmic consciousness and experienced a reality suddenly and perfectly, clearly seeing the intricacies of a rose pedal, or hearing the echo of a loon calling across a lake.

William Stafford in a charming poem called "Accepting Surprise" shows us one way to experience such manifestations:

The right mistake – the rich moment
when the rain finds you, a pinch
from a branch in the hedge that tells
you you're real, the wrong turn that
spills whole sunsets reflected and still
on a lake at a dead-end barring your road—

These are the doubled way, returns
even beyond dreams. Mothers, Fathers,
your lives flash into pain, and out;
but maverick rainbows blind us all. I bring
you—and your children—a whole treasure:
mistakes like jewels, the hidden rush
and loss of a world that throbs
beyond control, good, good, never quite ours.

This is one route and there are others. In the next chapters we shall examine more of them. The secret is to be open to these manifestations of "the timeless in time." Usually they are fortuitous, sometimes they are a serendipitous by-product of focusing, but always they are more than we expected, more than we could have hoped for. "The hidden rush/ and loss of a world that throbs/ beyond control, good, good, never quite ours."

EPIPHANIES

—〰—

A friend of mine built a house at the foot of the Sagua-ro National Monument in the Sonoran Desert east of Tucson. The place where she built the house was perilously close to a dry wash which raged like the Colora-do River when the August rains came. I asked her why she had chosen to build there, a dangerous place subject to flash floods. She told me that one day, after a desert storm had subsided, she saw a double rainbow that stretched across the horizon. She followed the rainbow to where its arc fell across a ridge and it was there that she decided to build.

There have been many rainbows since and she sees most of them right from her doorstep. The house is built in a most pre-carious spot but also in a most beautiful one. She has chosen to focus on the beauty, hope for a double rainbow (an occurrence hardly commonplace), and trust that if a disaster does occur, she will have the strength and the courage to meet it.

Probably it is the willingness to take risks which opens up opportunities for "maverick rainbows" in our lives. And these moments of intense awareness are certainly worth some risking, for it is through them that we transcend ourselves.

Epiphanies often clarify what is essential in our lives. In the words of T.S. Eliot:

> Man's curiosity searches past and future
> And clings to that dimension. But to apprehend
> The point of intersection of the timeless
> With time, is an occupation for the saint—

It is this apprehension of the point of intersection which is the focus of the epiphany. Eliot continues:

> No occupation either but something given
> And taken, in a lifetime's death in love,
> Ardour and selflessness and self-surrender.
> For most of us there is only the unattended
> Moment, the moment in and out of time,
> The distraction fit, lost in a shaft of sunlight,
> The wild thyme unseen, or the winter lightning
> Or the waterfall or the music heard so deeply
> It is not heard at all, but you are the music
> While the music lasts.

There are many kinds of recorded epiphanies, most in poetry or in a prose that rises to a lyrical evocation. Perhaps one day scholars will see the need of people to have them collected and bound in one sturdy volume that a man or woman could keep as a touchstone, a handbook for living, a key to unlocking the treasures of intense living. Now we must search through old chapbooks, magazines, and out-of-print poetry books. We must read a great deal of what we don't particularly find moving to find one or two gems.

Fortunately, the publishers of Wendell Berry's books have been luckier and more perceptive than most. Some of the best epiphanies in our language have been written by Berry and are readily available in his books published by Harcourt-Brace,

Best Cellar, Cold Mountain, and others. Here is a bit of one called "The Heron":

> There is another life than men have made.
> While summer's growth kept me
> anxious in planted rows, I forgot the river
> where it plowed, faithful to its way,
> beneath the slope where my household
> has taken its laborious stand.
> I could not reach it even in dreams.
> But one morning at the summer's end
> I remember it again...
> I go easy and silent, and the warblers
> appear among the leaves of the willows,
> their flight like gold thread
> quick in the live tapestry of the leaves.
> And I go on until I see a form crouched
> and I see the articulation of feather
> and living form, a brilliance I receive
> beyond my power to make, as he
> receives in his great patience
> the river's providence. And then I see
> that I am seen, admitted, my silence
> accepted in his silence...
> Suddenly I know that I have passed across
> to a shore where I do not live.

This is a holy moment; it is a moment in which Berry is blessed beyond all expectations. He has "passed across to a shore" where he does not live; he has apprehended the "point of intersection of the timeless with time."

Notice that in this poem Berry goes "easy and silent" down the river. He is not anxious for an intense experience; he is not imposing himself upon the pattern of life which is outside him. "Still as I keep, I might be a tree," Berry tells us earlier. There is a partial surrender of self here, the risk of letting go, of merging for a time within the larger life of the river. Finally, he notes that "my silence (is) accepted in his silence." Being quiet within is usually essential to having the kind of experience he describes. Eliot notes that for most of us who experienced this type of encounter "had the experience but missed the meaning." With Berry the experience becomes infused with meaning. The experience is revelation, incarnation, epiphany.

In another Berry poem entitled "The Silence" we see the crucial elements of risking self and going quietly into a silence that is even deeper that his own.

THE SILENCE

What must a man do to be at home in the world?
There must be times when he is here
as though absent, gone beyond words into the woven shadows
of the grass and their flighty darknesses
of leaves shaking in the wind, and beyond
the sense of weariness of engines and of his own heart,
his wrongs grown old unforgiven. It must be with him
as though his bones fade beyond thought...
... And then what presences will rise up
before him, weeds bearing flowers, and the dry wind
rain. What songs he will hear!

It is a shame that daydreaming is discouraged in the schools. Children need to loosen their minds of restraints, to pull away from the boredom of the curriculum as a car pulls out of congested traffic and goes speeding down the passing lane. We adults also need this as much as the children do, and our failure to recognize and fill this need in ourselves is probably responsible in part for the fact that we seldom tolerate it in our children's lives. Any loss of attention, any deviation into a world of daydreams is immediately suspect as Attention Deficit Disorder, as a "treatable" learning disability which the psycho-pharmaceutical professionals are more than ready to remedy with their prescriptions. Schools are for the most part as regimented and as ordered as prisons in this country and the cornucopia of pharmaceuticals are the trusted allies of the resident security guard.

We place too much emphasis both in our own lives and those of our children on learning segments of knowledge, on compartmentalizing data, on chopping our lives into periods of work, periods of study, periods of leisure. Sometimes I think that many of us forget that time itself is merely an abstraction, a unit of convenience with no reality at all outside that which we chose to give it. Time, which should be our servant, has become our master. At many schools the schedule is more important that the substance. I have seen administrators cut a humanities class which students had signed up for, or even an Advanced Placement course because it couldn't fit into the schedule. A perfect example of the cart coming before the horse.

In the workplace, too, this unswerving allegiance to the clock devalues both the individual and the nature of the work itself. Bound to this servitude of time (at least to all appearances) I've often taken great delight as a teacher in working harder at everything than was expected, of missing an occasional meal, of rising at two in the morning to work on a new lesson plan or an interdisciplinary class proposal. It is a kind of freedom. I have sought to combine classes with my colleagues: co-teaching joint seminars on biology and composition, research and biographical writing, psychology and contemporary fiction, physics and poetry. By resisting the segmenting effect of time, I feel that I am not only keeping my life whole, but I am overcoming the corrosive and divisive effect on the students of seeing learning as segmented and unconnected. *Everything is connected*, I tell my students. But it is not enough to simply tell them; they must experience it within the framework of the classroom. No easy task where schedules and segmented learning reign supreme.

To be able to step outside of time, to see—however briefly—the flow of life that is neither good nor bad, past or present, but is simply *now*, is not an easy thing to do whether you are bound to an institutional schedule or simply locked into the kind of everyday temporal mindset that enables you to catch trains on time, meet appointments, talk about growth, or improvement, or evolution.

Carl Sagan, the Princeton biologist and astronomer, called time the primary factor in the evolution of life on any planet. And if a major scientist thinks of time in this fashion, the reader might think my musings here presumptuous. But bear with me a moment.

What Sagan was focusing on is the developmental aspect of life. This is often quite necessary for a scientist. But the developmental aspect is but one facet: it does not define life and it certainly does not encompass life. It is an abstraction that limits as much as it increases our understanding of what life is. For Sagan's purposes, however, this abstraction was useful. For him to guess at the possibilities of life forms on other planets he had to proceed from the known (Earth) evolutionary development through time to the unknown (Mars).

This type of device is not only used by astronomers; it is a tool of social scientists as well. When we talk about what factors make juvenile delinquents or how they can be rehabilitated, we are speaking of things done to or imposed upon a particular human being at a particular point in time. But what is rarely discussed is the fact that the individual contains within himself *at all times* the potentiality for right action or for criminal action. The juvenile delinquent is potentially both the mature criminal and the judge upon the bench. Focusing on the individual as he or she appears now, we often lose sight of this fact. We become incapable of seeing this, in much the same way as a thirteen-year-old girl is incapable of seeing in her face the lines of a mature woman.

Richard Shelton's desert poetry is full of images about

stone. He speaks of "families of stones," of stones moving, living in the world. One would think, reading his work, that he actually believes stones are alive. And, in fact, they are. The pre-Cambrian rock was blue-green algae a billion years ago and will be something else a billion years from now. Outside of time it is always both what it was and what it is capable of becoming. The freckled-faced girl *is* the beautiful woman, *is* an old lady, *is* both embryo and corpse. Preoccupied with time she loses the immediacy of that perception. The temporary (temporal) fact of the rock robs us of the perspective from which Shelton writes so movingly, just as the temporary fact of puberty blinds the thirteen-year-old.

Herman Hesse once wrote that wisdom cannot be taught; it is not communicable in words. This is so because every truth must be expressed in narrow, dualistic terms. So, every truth is thus a half truth. And what seems absolute wisdom to some appears foolishness to others.

For both the resolution of opposites and the reality versus the abstraction of time, this statement is patently clear but less than obvious. That is why I have selected some epiphanies in this chapter to illustrate a way of *experiencing* these truths. They are not something that can be taught. They can only be absorbed by the individual in his or her own unique and particular way. And the ways of "apprehending the point of intersection of the timeless with time" are as varied as the ways of living or loving. They cannot be codified. And my way, or the ways I chose to illustrate in this book, are not truer or more certain than anyone else's. The epiphanies here are only "hints and guesses/ hints followed by guesses," as Eliot would say. They can lead the reader to a very special kind of enlightenment. But more likely they will merely point to the possibility of enlightenment and the reader will have to find his or her own way of going.

I spoke of the pre-Cambrian rock and of Shelton's desert

poetry. Perhaps a good place to leave this discussion on epiphanies would be with a poem by William Stafford, a poet who lived far from Shelton's desert but who knew, who had experienced, a similar illumination.

LIKE A LITTLE STONE

Like a little stone, feel the shadow of the great earth,
let distance piece you till you cling to trees.
That the whole world may be all the same
close your eyes until everything is…

If time won't let a thing happen, hurry there,
to the little end of the cone that darkness bends.
Any place where you turn but might have gone on,
all possibilities need you there.

FOURTH PLATEAU:
INTO ACTION

—ɱ—

The Welsh poet Dylan Thomas once wrote:

> The force that through the green fuse drives the flower
> Drives my green age; that blasts the roots of trees
> Is my destroyer.

As one moves from an understanding that there is an energy which infuses all life, and that we can access this energy and realize its power through self-forgetting, we also come to comprehend that we can utilize it to transform our lives. We come to see that this transformation can, in turn, have a powerful impact on the lives of others.

Of course, the same force that "drives our green age" also has the power to destroy. This is true of all energy: mechanical, electrical, nuclear. The same force that lights our homes has electrocuted unsuspecting victims, as well as (more purposely) convicted felons. The force that powers reactors in Europe and China, is also harnessed in the arsenals of many countries including one which has used it twice against civilian populations.

But the last line of the stanza quoted here is deceptive. Thomas, an alcoholic, saw the force as not only double-edged but destructive of himself. It was, he said, "my destroyer." But only in a truly positive sense is this true. As St. Francis wrote, "In dying we become born again to eternal life." It is through the death of the ego that this transformative energy infuses us, and we become new. And the energy itself is cannot die. Nor is this mere mythology, or Christian orthodoxy. It is a basic tenet of modern science and is reflected in both physics and chemistry. The Law of the Conservation of Energy states quite clearly, that the energy of any system remains constant; it is conserved over time. This law means that energy can neither be created nor destroyed; rather, it can only be transformed or transferred from one form to another. But more on this later.

The energy which we will be discussing in this chapter is real. It could be termed "psychological" energy as opposed to "physical," yet it has physical ramifications and effects. Also, since the word psychological comes from the root word *psyche* or soul, and has been connected with non-physical sources throughout history, I prefer calling it "spiritual" energy. I hope the reader will be open-minded and allow this term to be used without any prejudice. When I refer to spiritual energy, I mean that which comes from self-forgetting and then merging with a power outside of ourselves. It is a power that is available to us through mindfulness, focusing, concentration, or simply paying attention, when we let go of self-regard, self-consciousness, self-interest and preoccupation.

The Nicaraguan poet, Rubén Darío hints at it when he credits a Christian source in his "Little Poem for Jesus." He writes:

> Everything you ever said
> Can be summed up in two words:
> *Pay attention.*

And this attentiveness is what evokes or brings forth that power and allows it to infuse our lives. Through attention to a world outside of ourselves we become channels of that power, not the mere explosion at the end of a fuse, as Thomas suggests, which destroys the host, but rather a vital life-affirming conduit which can pass this energy on to others. And there is the secret of a long and fruitful life.

And for those patient readers who have been wondering what any of this has to do with Victor Frankl's *Search for Meaning*, or existential optimism, or any kind of philosophy, here is the answer. "The way forward," as Eliot wrote, "is the way back." This living as a channel of spiritual energy is the "point of intersection" when the history intersects with our present time and with future generations beyond our lives. This is where peak moments, flows, epiphanies, even world religions, Zen, and illumination come together into an engaged, truly alive, and conscientious way of life. But it will not come unless we work for it and that is the Fourth Plateau.

How on earth does one work for it, if the secret is self-forgetting and moving away from self-interest? Isn't having a goal-oriented "work ethic" in this process counterintuitive? No, not at all. Because what we are doing is developing a self which is transcendent so that one can be of service to others and add to the creative and healing energy in the world. That cannot be done without some concentration on those qualities which will aid in that mission. When we are on an airplane, we are reminded by the flight attendant that in case of an emergency and we are travelling with children, we must always put the oxygen mask **on ourselves first,** before we can help the child. Our attempt to assist the child might well prove futile if we ourselves are suffering from oxygen depletion. Likewise, we must consider work on our own psychic self-protection a prerequisite and make our own spiritual growth a priority.

Part of that work we are doing right now as we explore the connection between a life philosophy and experimental psychology, between peak moments and a life of intensity. Back to Eliot again:

> We had the experience but missed the meaning
> And approach to meaning restores the experience
> In a different form beyond any meaning we can as-
> sign to happiness.

Because what we are in search of, what we are working toward, is the openness, the attentiveness, the awareness, the readiness for "the hint half guessed, the gift half understood, [which] is Incarnation." This is when a spiritual potency infuses the body, or when the body transforms itself and unites with a more powerful force, a transcendent energy.

A final poetic example might illustrate how one man found through focusing, openness and self-forgetting, that moment of incarnation. In a lovely piece by James Wright called "A Blessing" which begins "just off the highway to Rochester Minnesota," the poet sees two Indian ponies in a pasture. He stops his car, on the side of the road, crosses the barbed wire and goes into the field. He notices how the eyes of the ponies "darken with kindness" as he approaches. One of the ponies trots over to him and nuzzles his hand. He caresses her long ear that is "delicate as the skin over a girl's wrist." Then, just then, and quite suddenly, he has a transcendent moment.

> Suddenly I realize
> That if I stepped out of my body
> I would break into blossom.

And here we see what the poet Marge Piercy calls the "Analogy of the Conservation of Energy" in poetry. Energy, as we mentioned before in our brief discussion of physics and chemistry, cannot be destroyed. It is merely converted from one form to another. So with this creative act of poetry.

First there was the inspiration of the poet, James Wright, when he felt his own transformation as he was on the verge of becoming one with the pony in the field, and all of nature around him, that he was about to "break" (dying to the self) "into blossom" (to be reborn in the spirit). This energy he then converted into the writing of the poem. The poem was then read and shared. And now a bit of it is in your mind, as it is in mine, operating with its transformative energy.

CREATING PATTERNS

—∿—

I was working at the American School in Guadalajara when the news was announced of the series of terrorist attacks on September 11, 2001. With so many of my colleagues and friends and family in the United States filled with grief, anger, with loss, I asked some of the students about their feelings as I walked around our campus. The results were predictable. "I feel like what happened was horrible," said one student. "I feel that whoever did this was not human," observed another. "I feel like this is a bad movie. I just can't believe it," said a third.

But does everyone see that these students were not expressing feelings at all? The students had put their feelings on hold. They were speaking in clichés, soundbites, vacuous phrases, circumlocutions. "I feel like this is a bad movie," is a simile, not a feeling. "I feel like what happened was horrible," is a descriptive statement, not a feeling. I feel like whoever did this was not human," is a hyperbole, not a feeling. The students were expressing thoughts, not emotions. They were distancing themselves from their feelings. Not one of the students I spoke with during the next day or two said he felt fear, panic, or nervousness, although these were things I knew the students felt. None said he felt anger or rage at those responsible. None said he or she felt sorrow or dismay at the enormous and meaningless waste of human life. Not one said she felt fragile, or vulnerable.

Why was that? Well, perhaps the poet William Stafford said it best, "I simply do not know," Stafford said, "exactly how I feel until I write it down. Often my feelings are contradictory, too nebulous; it is only writing that gives them substance."

When I pointed this out to my students a week later, and went through the process of listing, with their help, groups of emotions on the blackboard, they saw it clearly. Then, when I asked them to write a journal entry, the results were much more interesting. Not only for them, or for me as their teacher, but for all of us as a society. Because what happened is that the students not only wrote about their feelings, but how they became closer to their brother or little sister because they realized how fragile their lives were. One wrote about concern for the first time with her father flying up north on business, and how she loved him and never realized how much. Another wrote of a friend who was attending school in New York and how they had been like twins throughout their school careers in Guadalajara, and that she was determined that their friendship would go on, and not be destroyed as the twin towers in New York were. Another wrote in a prose reminiscent of Federico Garcia Lorca's poem *a las cinco de la tarde*, how the date of the tragedy in New York, the 11th of September, the 11th of September, the 11th of September would echo forever in her memory.

Finally, and this is perhaps the most poignant, one student wrote about how looking with her grandmother through old photo albums, the grandmother would always point out someone in a photo and say, "This was your great-aunt, she's dead now." Or point to an old building and say, "This used to be the store in Avenida Juárez, it's no longer there now. I don't remember when it was torn down." The student, her name was Ana Sofia, thought this was sad, something that happened when you got old.

But then she was looking through her own photo album with the pictures of her trip to New York the previous summer, the Twin Towers rising above Manhattan, and thinking how she would say to her own daughter one day, "They're no longer there now. But I remember the day when they came crashing down. They are a part of my history and it was a very sad time for all the world."

What the students did by this writing these passages in their journals was not only to express feelings, or affirm their love for friends and family, but they also created patterns, they created meaning out of chaos. They created a form out of formlessness, a meaning out of meaninglessness. They gave tragedy a shape. They defined **it** instead of letting it define them. It is something many of us have not yet managed to do, yet it is what we must do if we are to keep our balance, our integrity and our sense of rightness in the world. Revenge won't give us that, hatred won't give us that, nor will another century of military interventions give us that. Only our love for each other will provide us with meaning; only our caring will give shape to the chaos. And this love, this solidarity of human tenderness and hope, is the heart of all good teaching; it is what makes that profession one of the noblest of them all.

Our students were able to create images of the power of love and caring which replaced those on CNN of collapsing buildings; they sought understanding in the midst of rancor and bitterness. Students will always make such patterns provided we give them opportunities for social and emotional learning, whether it is in English class, or social studies, science, math, Spanish literature or computer science. Students who create patterns create meaning.

Dr. Victor Frankl, a survivor of the Nazi concentration camps was asked by someone what was the meaning of life. Now, here was a man who saw his family murdered by Nazis, his friends tossed into mass graves, the world he knew turned upside down during years and years of deprivation and torture when God seemed deaf, and life was without hope. "Asking me what the meaning of life is," Dr. Frankl said, "is like asking a chess master 'What is the best chess move?' There is no best move in chess; it depends on the circumstances of your game."

So, with the meaning of life, it depends on the circumstances of your life. "Therefore, the question of the meaning of life," Dr. Frankl says, "should be reversed. Ultimately, we should not ask what the meaning of life is but recognize that it is we who are being asked. Each of us is questioned by life, and we can only answer to life by answering for our actions; we respond to life by being responsible, and we create our own meaning through acts."

I think it is important to speak here of extreme situations which are the true test of life. Any religion, any philosophy, or even absence of one, will get us through the easy times. But when times get tough, I'd like the pragmatic teachings of a survivor from a Nazi death camp in my tool kit. Especially those of man who not only survived but went on to have a successful career in psychology, wrote books which changed people lives, and lived a life free of rancor and bitterness.

I know, because I have confronted those times of total failure, absolute grief and abandonment, how important the teaching of Frankl was for my survival. And I have learned over the years from my students, many of whom still write to me even after they have completed their education, how important this message has been for them. The message is simply: *No matter*

where you are, no matter what happens to you, you can always create meaning. And meaning is the substance of a successful life. No matter what else is going on in the world, no matter what your emotional state, if you chose to create a pattern, if you chose to create meaning, you will find peace and fulfillment.

FINDING YOURSELF AND OTHER MYTHS

—⟋⟍—

Octavio Paz writing in *The Labyrinth of Solitude* declares that in most societies people wear masks. In the Mexican society, he contends, because of a cultural legacy resulting from generations of Spanish colonialism and humiliation, most men have assumed the mask of the macho. To remove this mask, to show vulnerability, is dangerous since the core person would be revealed and the man would be open, womb-like. Openness is associated with the feminine, with weakness. The closed person, the "real" man, is hard and invulnerable.

So men in Paz's society are known only by the masks they wear in their daily occupations as politician, professor, business manager, or military officer, while the real person is buried somewhere no one can touch. As a result, Paz says, the intimacy which comes from true knowledge of a man is unavailable to his friends and to his family. The Mexican male is closed off, isolated, and inauthentic.

Much has been made of this description, not only of the Mexican male, but of many men—especially of a certain generation. I think Paz is mistaken, however, not so much in his observations but in his conclusions. I don't believe that the habits and disciplines we assume in our work result in most of us becoming inauthentic persons. I do not believe that the exterior person need be less than the whole person.

So many young people of the generation which came after Paz had so taken his ideas to heart and adopted the new solipsistic way of centralizing the interior life, that the phrases "search for the self", "finding out who you are," became part of everyday parlance. The question "What do you do for a living?" of my father's generation was less important than "Who are you really?"

We failed to realize that the question "What do you do? *is* the existential question. Who you are, cannot be separated from what you do. What one does may certainly include more than one's job or workday activities, but it must not fail to include them since they form a significant portion of one's daily activities. It is there that the interactions take place which test our views of who we are in the conflicts of relationships and values which form real life. It is there that our vision of ourselves is clarified or distorted by our actions.

For example, a young man or woman might hold the illusion that he or she is brave, but then behave cowardly on the field of combat. One might believe oneself to be a moral person but find oneself taking unfair advantage of a business client when the chance for a large profit appears. One might believe in tolerance and fairness but behave with a bias towards certain groups in society in one's role as an administrator or teacher. *It is only on the field of action that one can be truly authentic.* It is only when one puts on one of the masks that Paz complains of, that one's values and idealized self-image become concrete or that we fail to measure up.

Most people believe that they are better than they are, when in fact they are seldom better than they have to be. Honesty, tolerance, courage, generosity, and compassion are virtues which are developed or atrophied in the crucible of life, in relationships, in the give and take of our business, or our school, or profession. Often, we find that we fall far short of the good opinion we once had of ourselves; we make compromises which leave us much more diminished than that of our idealized selves.

I know a lieutenant who received the Navy Cross for bravery under fire. He rescued several fellow Marines after his platoon was decimated by mortar fire and then trapped by a sniper. What he later confessed to me, is that his sergeant was really responsible for the initial phase of the rescue, and that it was only after his non-com was killed that he, the lieutenant, broke from cover (where he was hiding and hoping to be presumed dead), found his men, and carried the wounded to safety. He was initially a coward in combat, afraid for his life. Later, shamed by the death of his sergeant, he was emboldened to make amends by stepping forward to rescuing the wounded. Those who benefited by his late but efficacious actions were grateful and contributed their witness statements to the battlefield report which resulted in his medal. But he knew that it was a born-again bravery. It is not my intention here to dismiss his bravery which was very real at the end. Even though it came late, it did come in time to save his men. But it was, I'm sure, far from his idealized courage as an untested young man.

I've worked both as a teacher and an administrator in overseas schools for more than thirty years. Mostly I worked with U.S. teachers in Latin America. Most of them came to the region not only for the sense of adventure but out of idealism as well. They wanted to make a difference in the world. They saw themselves as tolerant and moral people who held to a code of behavior and a set of standards which were of the highest order. And yet, in the day-to-day work of teaching, adjusting to a new culture, learning a new language, they made mistakes which were offensive to the constituency they served. I remember a science teacher from Texas working in Mexico who, when told to abide by a certain set of Mexican regulations complained: "Who are they to tell us what to do? They can't even drink their own water." She was an intelligent woman and a talented teacher. But her cultural fangs were showing, and her superior attitude alienated many of her Mexican colleagues.

I, too, was raised to be tolerant and open minded and I felt that these were the two most important factors in working abroad. I remember thinking that, of course their culture is different from ours, and that I needed to remember that different is not necessarily worse. But it never occurred to me that different is sometimes *better*, and that some of the students I would be teaching had a moral code superior to my own. I'm reminded of a story from my second year of teaching in Mexico when this feeling of superiority was replaced by one of deep humility. A student by the name of Nicolas Morris had arrived at my first period English class just minutes before the bell was to ring. He asked me for permission to go to the bathroom. "Go ahead," I said. "Just hurry back."

"Don't I need a pass," he asked.

"No, no," I said impatiently, anxious to begin my class. "Just go."

But our assistant principal at that time was quite severe. He gave detentions to students who were in the corridors without a pass. Anyway, the boy returned, quiet and seemingly depressed. I noticed, but I was in the middle of a lesson, so I made no comment. Later, I approached him. "What's going on, Nicolas? You look a bit down." "Nothing," he said, in the typical male fashion. So, I let it go until after class. When everybody had left

the room, I asked him again. "Come on, something's up, Nick. You were in a good mood this morning and now you're upset."

"Well," he said, "I just got a detention."

"For what?" I asked

"For being outside without a pass."

"But didn't you tell the vice-principal that it was my fault, that I didn't give you one?"

No," he said.

"Well, why not, Nicolas?"

"Because I didn't want you to get in trouble, Dr. Hogan.

Needless to say, I spoke to the vice principal and got him off the hook. But when I had time to reflect on the incident, I realized how humbled I was by this student's morals. As Pip said of Joe the Blacksmith in *Great Expectations*, "I looked up to him in my heart." To him it was more important that I not be hurt, than that he suffer an unjust detention. What an unselfish act! Even though I came from a good family and was educated at excellent schools in the U.S., I could not imagine myself capable of such a gesture as a teenager. It brought me humility, but it also revealed to me that some of my students in Mexico held themselves to an even higher standard of virtue and integrity than I had been used to in the United States. I realized that tolerance of a different culture was not the same as respect, and it was the latter I felt that day in the classroom.

A SURE HORIZON WILL COME AROUND YOU

—⟋⟍—

I mentioned earlier that being open means being vulnerable to the so-called "bad" feelings as well as the good or positive ones. For those who manage to survive the psychic assault of long incarceration, or survive the death of a loved one, or return from combat after a companion had fallen to an explosive roadside device, there will be guilt. Sometimes the guilt will have a real basis when we have, in fact, caused others pain, whether purposely or inadvertently. To deny that feeling would be to deny one's humanity.

But there is a second kind of guilt. If the first might be termed personal guilt, then the second might be called metaphysical guilt or *Weltschmertz*. This is the sadness, the shame that comes when we witness someone else's thoughtlessness, abuse, or even outright criminal act. When we share an awareness of someone else's violation of human solidarity, we are often ashamed *for* them. Frankl and his fellow prisoners experienced this each day in the concentration camps. There was also fear because these men also had the power of life and death over them. There was anger and frustration because no outlet existed for their anger which would not be self-destructive. And running through all these feelings was their shame at the Nazi captors' violation of human solidarity.

Both moral guilt and metaphysical guilt are both signs of psychic health. When teaching classes in prison, I remind the incarcerated students not to relax into quotidian contentment when soul-destroying forces are operating around them. While they should strive for tranquility, they should not forget that they have managed to survive while others have been lost to brutality, disease, or custodial indifference. They should never be content to move obliviously along without acknowledging their own responsibility to human solidarity.

Charles Fair, writing in The New Nonsense—The End of Rational Consensus, notes that:

> The impression one gets is that in this century we are using the whole highly developed apparatus of thought... to explain away... character and moral choice, which we have ceased to cultivate and therefore are ceasing to have. As the principle of individual responsibility becomes more and more problematical, we are forced, if only to save face, into devising theories which demonstrate that really those human attributes never existed...

Hypocrisy, contrary to the popular view is not disappearing among us. It is just becoming much easier, and assuming forms such as "sincerity" and "passion" which one can't quarrel with because they have almost no content. With the passing of traditional morality, we find we can dispense with the virtuosity once needed to put a good face on our actions.

In most extreme situations moral choices are simplified, and individual responsibility—while it may be denied—cannot be ignored. Unless one affirms life by accepting one's responsibility, not only to himself but to himself as a moral individual, he will eventually lose his identity and, in Terrence Des Pres's words, "lose faith in the capacity of goodness to prevail against the dehumanizing forces surrounding him."

Bruno Bettelheim, Frankl, and Des Pres, writing about survival in concentration camps, have referred to the danger of being so overwhelmed by the degradation of confinement, the brutality of prison life, the enormity of the forces of negation, that one tries to see it all as a dream in which one is both spectator and participant. There is a two-fold danger in this.

First, the sense of reality can become so pervasive that there is no resistance to death, no effort to protect one's life, no will to survive.

But there is a second and equally important danger. Often one begins to think of his life as a product of forces outside of himself, and that the acts of others as well as his own acts are not really his responsibility. He comes to believe that we are mere products of the forces of the world, of the system, or of fate. No one is to blame; it is no one's fault. The world is as the world is. Let go, and be guilt-free, anger-free and in harmony.

But this is to live a totally unexamined life and a completely irresponsible one. Guilt does not need to be a crippling emotion, nor does anger. Both can be liberating. We need to forgive ourselves of course and move on, but we do this first by acknowledging our guilt and making amends. We forgive others once justice has been satisfied. To do any less for ourselves or others would be to negate our accountability to ourselves and to others. It would be to renounce free will and with it our human dignity.

By accepting responsibility for our actions, by acknowledging guilt, we affirm our integrity as human beings. By acknowledging our shame at life-denying acts of others, we affirm life and our solidarity with other men.

Far from being negative, the effect of such acknowledgement is that of psychic revival. It enables us to confront negative forces with courage and real strength. It enables us to face with a clear gaze and unashamedly all those who would deny the life-affirming instincts in us and in others. For it is finally our human dignity, a self-conscious, self-determining faculty whose function is to insist upon its own integrity, which enables us to pass through the consciousness of our separation from humanity to an affirmation of our unity.

The greatest shame of all is the inability to acknowledge guilt. And there is perhaps no greater injustice than self-deception. But when we acknowledge our responsibility to life, darkness has no power to reduce us. Having been true to ourselves there is no existential shame. In this light it seems appropriate to quote from Wendell Berry's beautiful poem:

> You will be walking some night
> in the comfortable dark of your yard
> and suddenly a great light will shine
> round about you, and behind you
> will be a wall you never saw before.
> It will be clear suddenly
> that you were about to escape,
> and that you are guilty, you misread
> the complex instructions, you are not
> a member, you lost your card
> or never had one...
> Though you have done nothing shameful,
> they will want you to be ashamed.
> They will want you to kneel and weep
> and say you should have been like them.
> and once you say that you are ashamed,
> reading the page they hold out to you,
> then such light as you have made
> in your history will leave you.
> There is no power against them.

It is only candor that is aloof from them,
only an inward clarity, unashamed,
that they cannot reach. Be ready.
When their light has picked you out
and their questions are asked, say to them:
"I am not ashamed." A sure horizon
will come around you.

"It is only candor that is aloof from them," from those who would destroy our integrity, from those who would have us exchange our self-determination for the security of their creed, or system, or politics. We must acknowledge our guilt when there is a real basis for it, and then make amends, ask for forgiveness from those we have injured, and then forgive ourselves. We must face the collective guilt of actions done in our name whether preemptive war or capital punishment, and seek to replace bombing with negotiated peace, and retribution with rehabilitative justice. Only acceptance of our personal and collective responsibility ultimately allows us to be unashamed, to walk with a sure horizon, with the inward clarity of a good conscience and existential integrity.

THE NAME OF THE PLACE IS LOVE

—m—

Ralph Waldo Emerson in his memorable essay on self-reliance noted that "as men's prayers are a disease of the will, so are their creeds a disease of the intellect…Everywhere I am hindered from meeting God in my brother, because he has shut his own temple doors." Emerson goes on to say that we must stop "repeating fables of our brother, or our brother's God" and realize that "every new mind is a new classification."

This last phase contains the essence of existential optimism. "Every new mind is a new classification." From the pre-Socratics to Alan Watts, philosophy has been an individual realization of collective potential. But we as individuals can expect little in the way of such realization if we simply and uncritically accept the views of any single philosophy no matter how brilliant and well-reasoned, and become Aristotelians, Platonists, Theists, Kantians, Marxists or whatever. If philosophy is to help us to become more truly ourselves (and to realize our immense potential) we must avoid being seduced into membership of any school, sect, or cult. We must refuse to surrender our minds to someone else's conceptions.

What these various philosophies can do is show us some avenues which have already been traveled and where the roadblocks are, and which of these routes is still under construction. The value of such intellectual roadmaps should not be underestimated. They can save us much in terms of time and misdirected thought.

Existentialism is one of the more recent of philosophical attempts to gather as many elements of human reality as possible into a total picture of what it means to be human. However, there are still many elements which have not been fully resolved and may never be fully incorporated into a unified theory. They need to be discussed here because they are precisely the factors which deal with the central concern of life's meaning.

The first element is faith. By faith I do not mean the outworn creeds or dogmas, or even the philosophical disciplines. I mean what my child demonstrates when she believes that I will do what I have promised her that I would do. In this context faith is essentially trust. She trusts me to do precisely what I have said I am going to do.

Philosophically, faith is in much disrepute. But in actuality it is the *sine qua non* of any philosophy which aims to gather the diverse elements of human reality into a total picture. I am not speaking here of positivistic or scientific faith, i.e., that everything is ultimately knowable. I mean simply faith in oneself, trusting yourself and the pattern of your life. It is within this pattern that meaning exists.

Victor Frankl tells us *in Man's Search for Meaning* that:

> .... the meaning of life differs from man to man, from day to day, from hour to hour. What matters therefore, is not the meaning of life in general but rather the specific meaning of a person's life at a

given moment.

So, if one is to use the way of philosophy (or meditation or yoga or mind control, for that matter) as a means of finding the meaning of life, he must first begin with trust in himself; himself as the final critic of learning, himself as final arbiter of perception, himself as final recipient of all meaning.

But often we must go outside ourselves to find ourselves. It is a necessary expedient since we are social animals who we live in the world and that is the laboratory in which we must discover ourselves. And the discovery is never final. It is continuous. We are forever discovering, forever revising ourselves, forever searching for meaning, and each day is as much as a thousand years of life since each day of life is a point of light in a continuous pattern woven throughout all time, water in a stream which is always flowing.

So, faith in ourselves means, ultimately, faith in that extension of ourselves which is all that we are and all that we are becoming. It means faith in the pattern of our life on this planet.

The critical reader might now be saying: He is telling us nothing new, nothing we have not already heard. His is quoting Emerson's "Self Reliance" and Frankl's *Man's Search for Meaning* and giving us nothing original. And to that criticism I can only reply that I have thrown out the chaff of Emerson and retained only the wheat for this eclectic view. The wheat in this case, the core of his thought, is self-trust. And it is not something which I discovered in Emerson or in the pages of any book. Rather, it is something I found in my own life after many wearisome and self-destructive years and then found ratified in his simple essay.

But this knowledge, which is now mine and was his, is not esoteric knowledge to be footnoted in a philosophical text. It is collected knowledge that is continuously forgotten and needs to be continuously discovered again in the different lives and new contexts of each succeeding generation. Quite simply it is this: Trust yourself. Trust the pattern of your life.

If primary faith is the first element of existential optimism, the second element is love. Few philosophies consider this second element an integral part of their systems. And it is precisely this omission which leads to philosophic nihilism, to a devaluation of life and knowledge.

It seems to me that life cannot be seen as inherently precious unless there is an affirmation of life, unless we see something outside of ourselves as being worthy of respect and affection. Some people love easily and other not. This ease or lack of it has much to do with trust, the first element discussed in this chapter. One cannot love himself unless he trusts himself; that should be obvious. Equally he cannot love others if he does not first love himself.

Faith proceeds love. If I am uncertain whether I will do something petty or repulsive or self-destructive, it is clear that I am not in much of a position to love myself. But having established that I have responsibility for the organism which is me, I come to respect myself and value myself. Beyond that, I learn to respect and value the "otherness" of certain individuals, along with their grace, their beauty, and their intelligence. I value the differences which define them. To the extent that I can value that otherness, to the extent that I am filled with that otherness while still being me, I am in love.

Sometimes when my son was still a young boy and his death beyond imagining, we would take long walks in the Sonoran Desert, and talk quietly. Sometimes we would stop as I pointed out a cactus wren on a saguaro, or a kangaroo rat hiding in a creosote bush. Our mutual discoveries of the natural world and the naming of them filled him with delight. Even more exciting for him was rethinking the design of our cities to try to accommodate the natural world.

I'd like to design a biosphere in which every
animal had its place and man was just one of the
many animals. Wouldn't that be cool? Instead of
urban design like they do now of cities that are
based on man, mine would be based on animals
and would have deserts and forests and even
beaver dams in the creeks behind the houses.

—Gary's Journal

I was so filled with the presence of his otherness that I
wanted to reach out and hug him. Sometimes I did. His eyes,
his chin, were so much like mine. His smile, exactly like his
mother's. But he was no carbon copy of his mother or of me.
He was unique and quintessentially other.

Although I was fascinated by the way his young mind
worked, and his enthusiasm for new knowledge, these were not
the reasons I loved him. I loved him without reason, beyond
reason. Reason, however, told me that because he was Other,
there would be a time for letting go. I knew I could not hold
him forever or even perhaps for most of my lifetime. Each time
I did hold him I knew with a sinking heart that as he grew
older these quiet times together would be fewer and fewer. On
special days when I was conscious of the transitory nature of
life and its beauty, I even stopped to consider that this time
might be the last.

And it was precisely this knowledge or foreknowledge
which brought such intensity to the times we were together.
And just as it is the inevitability of letting go brings meaning to
our embrace, so it is death which invests life with meaning.

How utterly devoid of ambition or lust for life we would
be if we thought we had forever to live. Everything could wait
until tomorrow. There would be no risk, no adventure. The
fragility of life which so many of us lament is in actuality the
foundation of human happiness.

Happiness cannot exist in a vacuum and only a fool is always happy. Yet many people are taught by parents, by school and by the media that they have a right to be happy. They become convinced that there is something wrong with them if they are not happy. And this has a domino effect. One goes from being sad, to feeling depressed about the sadness, then to feeling alienated from a world which is so indifferent to that sadness, then to distrusting the organism for not rising above the external events, and ultimately to despair.

But pain and sadness are essential to happiness. Unless one experiences the feeling of thirst, he cannot fully appreciate the taste of pure spring water. Unless one knows or can vividly imagine what it is to lose someone he loves or to suffer a serious illness, he cannot fully appreciate the wonder of a human life, or glory in the fullness of health. Deprivation sharpens our senses and suffering our sensitivity.

My first experience with the death of a child occurred when my neighbor's a twelve-year-old son was involved in a motocross accident. A high-tension wire burned the child's face, and his arm was cut off when the wire snapped against his shoulder. The boy was exactly my son's age then and, besides being crippled by the accident, he was terribly scarred. I followed the boy's progress in the hospital each day. I spoke to his father and tried to be supportive. Always, in the back of my mind was the thought: *This could have been my son.* Then, just as the father had come to terms with his son's physical scarring and lost limb, the boy took a turn for the worse. A swift progressive infection set in and the child died. *This could have been my son,* I thought, looking at his tiny corpse at the funeral home and I knew then that every escape from the perils of childhood was a narrow one.

I knew then that no matter what parents do, no matter how much they love their children, or how many survival skills

they give them; there is still the possibility of the freak accident, the crippling illness, the error in judgment. Everything we fathers and mothers do, everything we should or might do, can never, with any real certainty, be enough. Human life is fragile, and we are not guardian angels. And certainly, it is partly this which makes the time we do have with our children so precious; the fact that tomorrow they might not be here, or that we ourselves might not see the new day.

It is unfortunate that some people choose to focus on the negative aspect of mortality: *What's the use*, they say, *we all arrive at the same destination*—and not the positive aspect: the joy of the journey itself. It is the very fact of death which makes our lives so precious. And the annoying way it has of announcing itself at the most inopportune times should give our lives intensity, not rob them of purpose. Death is what makes love possible. "Here we are," writes Lucille Clifton:

> running with the weeds
> colors exaggerated
> pistil wild
> embarrassing the calm family flowers
> oh
> here we are
> flourishing for the field
> and the name of the place
> is Love

LIVING IS NO
LAUGHING MATTER

—◦◦◦—

have quoted a great deal of contemporary poetry in the
foregoing chapters. I have done this because unless existential optimism is seen in the context of particular human
lives and particular situations, it appears simplistic, perhaps
even banal. The works I have chosen to quote, as diverse as
they all are, do have one thing in common: the heightened
sense of awareness out of which they were written. And each
is as individual as the lives of the poets themselves, lives which
are—all things considered—no more remarkable than your
life or mine.

Joseph Brodsky in an essay once noted that he did not see
why poems, short stories and novels were all considered different forms. "Surely a novel, if it is any good, is a poem: so, too, a
short story." And perhaps it is the heightened awareness, their
intensity of language, more than the form itself which makes
certain kinds of writing poetry. At any rate these are the qualities which have brought me to rely so heavily in this book on

certain quoted passages from the works of contemporary poets to illustrate some ways in which one might live authentically and with faith.

Seeing the elements which we have discussed in actual lives, tested in the kiln of human experience, gives us a clearer awareness of the possibilities of our own lives if we recognize the value of these elements and allow them to develop free of fear, distrust and self-contempt.

Walt Whitman, speaking of what a poet should be, wrote that "he is complete in himself... the others are as good as he, only he sees it and they do not." Then, speaking to men and women everywhere, he advised:

> Love the earth and the sun and the animals...
> Take off your hat to nothing known or unknown
> or to any man or number of men, go freely with
> powerful uneducated persons and with the young
> and with the mothers of families... reexamine all
> you have even been told at school or church or in
> any book, dismiss what insults your own soul, and
> your very flesh shall be a great poem and have the
> richest fluency....

This is the faith of which we spoke in the preceding chapter; the trust in oneself as final arbiter to "dismiss what insults your own soul." But Whitman does not stop there. Self-trust, self-reliance are barren qualities without more. I am reminded in this context of a cartoon I once saw in which a lovely Greek girl was tugging on the arm of a handsome Greek lad who was examining his reflection in the water. The girl asked plaintively, "Tell me, Narcissus. Is there someone else?" And, of course, for Narcissus as for so many others there is no one else, and nothing else but himself. So, Whitman continues his description of what a poet should be:

> The known universe has one complete lover and
> that is the greatest poet. He consumes an eternal
> passion and is indifferent which chance happens
> and which possible contingency of fortune or
> misfortune and persuades daily and hourly his
> delicious pay. What balks or breaks others is
> the fuel for his burning progress to contact an
> amorous joy. Nothing can jar him...suffering and
> darkness cannot—death and fear cannot. To him
> complaint and jealousy and envy are corpses
> buried and rotten in the earth...he saw them
> buried. The sea is not surer of the shore or the
> shore the sea than he is of the fruition of his love...

Marge Piercy in her aptly titled poem "We Become New" illustrates the incredibly heightened awareness which love brings to our lives. We spoke of focusing, of philosophy, of attitude, as ways of becoming new. But love can make the leap far more quickly than such disciplines, although without such disciplines its staying power is limited. Piercy in this vivid poem clearly shows the sensual power and the fragility of love:

> How it feels to be touching
> you: an Io moth, orange
> and yellow as pollen,
> wings through the night
> miles to mate,
> could crumble in the hand....
> When I am turning slowly
> in the woven hammocks of our talk
> when I am chocolate melting into you
> I taste everything new
> in your mouth.

And this is what it is all about, this kind of awareness in which we see and feel and taste everything new again and find wonder and joy and mystery in the mere fact of existence.

Contemporary poetry is a place where such experiences are

recounted, where one can see the elements not in the abstract but in the concrete reality of a particularly human life. If it is well-written, if it is authentic and honest, it is one of the best resources available to existential optimist. One of the most moving examples is this one by Nazim Hikmet, a political prisoner who spent seventeen years confined to a maximum-security cell in Turkey before he was finally released in a general amnesty. He later received the Nobel Peace Prize.

ON LIVING

I

Living is no laughing matter:
you must live with great seriousness
like a squirrel, for example—
I mean without looking for something above and
beyond living.
I mean living must be your whole occupation.
Living is no laughing matter:
…I mean you must take living so seriously
that even at seventy, for example, you will
plant olives—
and not so they'll be left for your grandchildren either
but because even though you fear death you don't
believe it,
because living, I mean, weighs heavier.

II

Let's say we're seriously ill, need surgery—
which is to say that there a chance we won't get up
from the white table.
Even though it's impossible not to feel sad about
going a little too soon,
we'll still laugh at the jokes being told,
we'll look out the window to see if it's raining
or we'll wait anxiously
for the latest newscast….
Let's say we're in prison
and close to fifty,

and we have eighteen more years, say, before the
iron doors will open.
we'll still live with the outside,
with its people and animals, struggle and wind—
I mean with the outside beyond the walls.
I mean, however and wherever we are,
we must live as if one never dies.

III

This earth will grow cold,
a star among stars
and one of the smallest—
a gilded mote on the blue velvet, I mean,
I mean this, our great earth.
The earth will grow cold one day,
not like a heap of ice
or a dead cloud even,
but like an empty walnut it will roll along
in pitch black space…
You must grieve for this right now,
for the world must be loved this much
if you're going to say, "I lived"… .

So many of the elements we have been discussing are contained
in this poem and presented in concrete terms. It is precisely
the seriousness of life that enables is to laugh at the jokes before being wheeled into surgery to undergo an operation from
which we may not recover. It was precisely Hikmet's loss of
freedom which made him so value and honor it in his lifetime.

Often people speak of freedom as if it is something that
the benevolence of the government permits us to have. But the
contrary is true. Most governments are either indifferent to
individual freedom or, as Hikmet clearly discovered, outright
hostile to it. Much of what is real freedom, however, can be
attained even in the most repressive regimes. It is internal, in-
dependent of the walls or those who build and maintain them.

I wrote earlier of focusing and of the importance of keeping in mind that no matter what the situation, we can choose a certain response to it, choose to see it one way rather than another, focus on its affirmative possibilities rather than on its negative ones.

But I do not wish to imply that such emotions such as fear, anger, remorse, guilt have no place in the life of the existential optimist. They are often true indicators of our psychic health and our acute awareness of the world and our place in it. We should feel anger when we are treated unjustly; we should feel fear when our organism is in danger; we should feel guilt when parallel lives have paid a price that enable ours to continue; remorse, when we did not act as we should have acted, or remained silent when we should have spoken out.

It is not the experience of guilt or fear which defines an individual in an extreme situation, any more than it is the sensory deprivation, the atmosphere of violence, or even the numbness of institutional life which define a man in prison. Rather, it is the direction of one's life towards harmony which is the determinant, and in that direction even negative elements play a significant role.

Bruno Bettelheim, another former prisoner of the Nazi death camps, has written a great deal on what the survivors brought out of that experience. He notes that:"

> From not having enough space to lie down at night, from living in starvation, the survivor… learned that even under such conditions, one can discover a life of harmony which permits one to make do, to get along with others, and to live in harmony with oneself.

In an age where mere physical survival is much touted, I think this comment from a concentration campy survivor is extremely significant. Living is truly "no laughing matter" and there are serious risks one must take to retain a quality of life consistent with one's authenticity. There were Jews, for example, at Dachau and Buchenwald who could have survived if they chose to abuse or inform on their fellow prisoners. There were Jewish doctors who could have avoided or postponed their death indefinitely if they had chosen to exercise their medical skills in the service of the Third Reich. Electing not to do these things required great courage. But others, like Bettelheim, were not put to these kinds of tests. And the knowledge that their survival was due only to the luck of the draw (not having been tested in the same ways as those who died) was often a cause for guilt.

Interestingly enough (for armchair philosophers who would explain guilt away and have the ex-prisoners forget and learn to adjust), it is precisely this knowledge and the guilt that accompanied it which gives meaning to the survivor's life and gives survival its value. As Bettelheim sums up:

> Our experience did not teach us that life is meaningless, that the world of the living is but a whore house, that one ought to abide by the body's crude claims, disregarding the compulsion of culture. It taught us that miserable although the world in which we live may be, the difference between it and the world of the concentration camps is as great as that between night and day, hell and salvation, death and life. It taught us that there is a meaning to life, difficult though that meaning is to fathom—a much deeper meaning than we had thought possible before we became survivors. And our feeling of guilt at having been so lucky as to survive is a most significant part of this meaning—testimony to a humanity that not even the abomination of the concentration camps can destroy.

Some might consider the discussion of such extreme situations completely irrelevant to life as they encounter it on a day-to-day basis. These desperate questions of meaning, of value, of authenticity do not concern them. But sooner or later, each of us is in a place where these questions must be faced if we are truly said to have lived. And what happens then will depend upon what one professes to believe and one's courage to live out his or her own definition of self. As Frankl writes:

> As each situation in life represents a challenge to man and presents a problem for him to solve, the question of the meaning of life may actually be reversed. Ultimately A mAn should ask not what the meaning of life is, but rather recognize that it is he who is being asked. In a word, each man is questioned by life; and he can only answer to life by answering for his own life; to life he can only respond by being responsible.

Many of us are survivors because we have never been tested. And for us the ultimate test may be simply endurance, a test that should not (for all its seeming banality) be treated casually. For in meeting that test with seriousness, with patience, and courage, there is the ultimate opportunity for the creation of meaning. And now, here is a prose poem by Greg Kuzma which is a fitting illustration of this point and an appropriate note with which to conclude this chapter.

LET THERE BE AN END TO EXCUSES

When you are old and defeated and your elbows protrude from your clothes like so many drunken football fans, say you are learning from experience the price of victory. When you are old, and your few teeth are your last few friends, say it is OK there is more room now in your mouth for your tongue when before there was never enough space to echo its fine speeches. When you are old, and your skin bags on you like trousers on the clothesline in the wind, say rather that beauty is not skin deep... . And when you are old, and the lights

dim in both your eyes, and your eyeglasses are heavy as barbells, and your hands are brown and twisted as dead wasps, say instead of the usual "I count the days," that you are ready to deal the cards, ready to put the pot on, to call time out so that you can come back into the game.

POSTSCRIPT: IN TIME OF THE CORONAVIRUS

—⁓—

As I work on the final edit of this book, the coronavirus, now known as COVID-19, has devastated the populations of several countries, crippled the world economy, and forced us to stay indoors in a kind of involuntary incarceration. Although I could not have anticipated this crisis when I began this book several years ago, it is both heartening and unsettling to see how deeply relevant to life these pages are. Under trying circumstances of isolation and uncertainty, many of us feel compelled to search for assurances in our lives.

I was motivated today after a short walk in the neighborhood park (early morning before others were out for exercise) to go back and re-read William Wordsworth's beloved "Lines Composed Above Tintern Abbey." The poem, you may recall, was written after the poet hiked up to the old ruin of the abbey on the banks of the Wye River in England. Amazingly, he wrote the entire piece in one draft (with no additions or cross-outs) on arriving back from his walk. He had been to this forested area before as a youngster, and was energized by the waterfall, the deep river, and the lonely streams as he meandered along the rustic trail. He wrote:

> The sounding cataract
> Haunted me like a passion: the tall rock,
> The mountain, and the deep and gloomy wood,
> Their colours and their forms, were then to me
> An appetite; a feeling and a love
> That had no need of a remoter charm…

But now "that time is past." He is a much more mature and sedate man when he returns. *Here he faces the reality of his life unflinchingly. This is the First Plateau.* He is considerably older and no longer the hearty hiker oblivious to anything but the flow of his blood, the rush of the waterfall, and the glad animal movement and responses of his muscles. Now, as he stops occasionally to catch his breath, he enters into a more thoughtful and contemplative mood, and realizes, nevertheless, there is "abundance recompense" for this loss of youth, for in this moment "there is life and food for future years." *He has arrived at the Second Plateau: gratefully affirming that which is, and flowing with it, assigning a meaning to it.*

> For I have felt
> A presence that disturbs me with the joy
> Of elevated thought: a sense sublime
> Of something far more interfused,
> Whose dwelling is the light of setting suns,
> And the round ocean and the living air,
> And the blue sky, and in the mind of man.
> A motion and a spirit, that impels
> All thinking things, all objects of all thought
> And rolls through all things.

And here he has arrived at the Third Plateau: realizing that there is another world and that it is in this one. It is an awareness that might be called spiritual. It is an awakening to the possibilities of life which are endless in this every moment is eternity. Now all that remains, is how this awareness can lead to a more fruitful life, not only for the poet but for others. It begins with the understanding that this experience of transcendence

> ...can so inform the mind that is within us, so impress
> With quietness and beauty, and so feed
> With lofty thoughts, that neither evil tongues,
> Rash judgements, nor the sneers of selfish men,
> Nor greetings where no kindness is, nor all
> The dreary intercourse of daily life,
> Shall e'er prevail against us, or disturb
> Our cheerful faith, that all which we behold
> Is full of blessings.

And so this poem which was originally for his sister Dorothy ("my dear, dear Sister") is really for all of us all. It is Wordsworth's gift to us, his service to mankind which is *the Fourth Plateau: to add to the creative and healing energy of the world.* He ends with the hope that her mind (and—by extension— our minds as well)

> Shall be a mansion for all lovely forms
> Thy memory be as a dwelling-place
> For all sweet sounds and harmonies: oh! then,
> If solitude, or fear, or pain, or grief,
> Should be thy portion, with what healing thoughts
> Of tender joy will through remember me
> And these my exhortations!

Sitting in my garden in Mexico while the news media, the Internet, and even the phone apps scream death from a plague which has infested every nook and cranny of the world, I quietly read these "Lines Composed a Few Miles above Tintern Abbey, On Revisiting the Bank of the Wye during a Tour. July 13, 1798." They are lines which comfort me and assure me that acceptance is the key to tranquility, as the doves call across the hillside, and spring announces a rebirth in the lemon sunshine of jonquils and the purple blush of jacaranda.

Colonia Providencia
Guadalajara, Jalisco
May, 2020

NOTES, COPYRIGHT INFORMATION, AND FURTHER READING

—ꟿ—

I n this volume I have quoted literally from many books, especially from those of poets whose work has influenced me over the years and who provide touchstones for many of the themes described within. In each case, I have provided the name of the book and the publication details below in the order in which they appear. Some of these such as the poems of John Milton and William Wordsworth are obviously in the public domain. Other are quoted under the provisions of "fair usage" and I hope will encourage readers to see these excerpts as mini reviews as the author's work and that they will go on to read more.

FIRST PLATEAU

Chosen Place by Richard Shelton. Copyright ©1975 by Richard Shelton. Best Cellar Press, 1975.

Being and Nothingness by Jean Paul Sartre. Copyright ©1943 by Jean Paul Sartre. Philosophical Library, 1956.

The New World by Fred Turner. Copyright ©1975 by Fred Turner. Ilium Press, 1975.

"Maybe" by *Miklós Radnóti, from Miklós Radnóti. The Complete Poetry in Hungarian and English*. Copyright © 2014 Gabor Barabas (trans.) and Miklós Radnóti. McFarland and Co.

THE SECOND PLATEAU

"A Ritual to Read to Each Other by William Stafford from *Stories Which Could be True. Copyright* © 1977, 1982 by the Estate of William Stafford. Harper-Collins, 1982.

Paradise Lost. John Milton. Public Domain (1667).

ALCOHOL AND DRUGS

The Birth of Tragedy by Friedrich Nietzsche. (Public Domain. (1872).

Confessions of An Opium Eater by Thomas DeQuincy. Public Domain (18210.

Doors of Perception & Heaven and Hell by Aldous Huxley. Public Domain. 1954).

The Psychedelic Experience by Timothy Leary and Richard Metzner. Copyright © 1964 by Timothy Leary and Richard Metzner. University Books, 1964.

The Teachings of Don Juan: A Yaqui Way of Knowledge by Carlos Castaneda. Copyright © 1968 by Carlos Castaneda. University of California, Press, 1968.

COMBAT HIGH

Fear: A Cultural History by Joanna Burke. Copyright © 2015 by Joanna Burke. Virago, 1975.

RECOVERY

The Variety of Religious Experience by William James. Public Domain (1902)

Pragmatism: A New Name for Some Old Ways of Thinking by William James. Public Domain. (1907).

FOCUSING

Personal letter to the author from John Paul Minarik. Permission to quote from with attribution gratefully acknowledged. ca. 1975.

Unpublished journal of J. Charles Green. Inherited by the author after Green's death in prison, ca. 1974.

The Portrait of Dorian Grey by Oscar Wilde. Public Domain.

"Whatever" by Eugène Guillevic. Quote passage from Savory, Teo. "An Introduction to Guillevic." *Books Abroad* 45, no. 1 (1971): 43-45. Accessed September 21, 2020. doi:10.2307/40125008.

"Canticle" by Joseph Bruchac from *Flow*. Copyright ©1975 by Joseph Bruchac. Greenfield Review Press, 1975.

"Accepting Surprise" by William Stafford originally appeared in the *The Hampden-Sydney Poetry Review,* 1974. Copyright © 1974, 1982 by the Estate of William Stafford.

EPIPHANIES

"Four Quarters" by T.S. Eliot. *Collected Poems 1909-1962.* Copyright ©1963 by T.S. Eliot. Harcourt, Inc. 1963.

"The Heron" and "The Silence" by Wendel Berry. From *The New Collected Poems*, Copyright ©1974, 2012 by Wendell Berry. Counterpoint, 2012.

"Like A Little Stone" by William Stafford. Copyright ©1974 by William Stafford. From a broadside published by Turkey Press, 1975.

FOURTH PLATEAU: INTO ACTION

"The force that through the green fuse drives the flower" by Dylan Thomas. From the *Collected Poems of Dylan Thomas, 1934-1952*. Copyright ©1952 by Dylan Thomas. Everyman's Library, 1966.

"Little Poem for Jesus" by Rubén Darío. "Pequeña poema para

POSTSCRIPT: IN THE TIME OF CORONAVIRUS

Other books by Michael Hogan

Guns Grit and Glory: How the US and Mexico Came Together to Defeat the Last Empire in the Americas **2019**

Abraham Lincoln and Mexico: A History of Courage, Intrigue and Unlikely Friendships **2016**

Abraham Lincoln y México: Un Relato de Valentía, Intriga y Amistades Improbables. Spanish Edition **2016**

In the Time of the Jacarandas **2015**

A Metaphorical Piano and Other Stories **2013**

A Lion at a Cocktail Party, 35th Anniversary Edition **2013**

The Irish Soldiers of Mexico **2011**

Los Soldados Irlandeses de México (Spanish Edition), **2012**

Molly Malone and the San Patricios **2011**

Molly Malone Y Los San Patricios (Spanish Edition) **2012**

Winter Solstice **2012**

Newport: A Writer's Beginnings **2012**

A Death in Newport **2011**

Imperfect Geographies **2011**

Teaching from the Heart: Essays and Speeches on Teaching at American Schools in Latin America **2011**

Intelligent Mistakes **2011**

Twelve Habits of the Creative Mind, **2011**

A Writer's Manual For Inmates in Correctional Institutions **2011**

Savage Capitalism and the Myth of Democracy **2009**

Mexican Mornings **2006**

Making Our Own Rules: New and Selected Poems **1989**

The broken face of summer: Poems **1981**

Rust **1977**

Risky Business **1977**

Soon it will be morning **1976**

Letters For My Son **1975**

CPSIA information can be obtained
at www.ICGtesting.com
Printed in the USA
BVHW050900200323
660780BV00014B/1030

9 798695 046571